The Crisis

with cartoons by Phil Evans

TONY CLIFF
THE CRISIS
SOCIAL CONTRACT
OR SOCIALISM

Pluto   Press
for Socialist Worker

by Tony Cliff:

Rosa Luxemburg, 1959
Incomes Policy, Legislation and Shop Stewards, 1966
(with Colin Barker)
France, the Struggle Goes On, 1968
(with Ian Birchall)
*The Employers' Offensive: Productivity Deals and How
to Fight Them*, 1970
State Capitalism in Russia, 1974
Lenin, Volume 1: *Building the Party*, 1975

First published 1975 by
Pluto Press Limited,
Unit 10 Spencer Court,
7 Chalcot Road,
London NW1 8LH

ISBN 0 902818 75 9

Cover design by Katerina Antoniou

Cover photo by Peter Harrap

Cover: 17 October 1974. British Leyland bus and
truck workers at the AEC Factory in Southall hear
shop stewards recommend the rejection of
management's latest offer.

Printed in Great Britain by
Redwood Burn Limited
Trowbridge & Esher

Contents

Acknowledgements

Many members of the International Socialists contributed to this book. Much of what they had to say appeared in *Socialist Worker* and *International Socialism;* some was written specially. I also took a great deal from a number of rank and file papers: the *Carworker,* the *Dockworker, Rank and File Teacher, Redder Tape, NALGO Action,* the *Hospital Worker,* the *Collier* and others.

I am especially grateful to Mike Kidron whose unstinted work sharpened both the style and the argument.

Tony Cliff
London
1 November 1974

Introduction:
Prophecies of Doom

The press and television, politicians of all parties, economics experts – everyone – are telling us that the world is drifting into the most serious economic crisis since the 1930s.

In Britain the Court Line has collapsed, Ferranti has asked for bail, Jessel Securities is being propped up. Dozens of other companies are in a similar position. In September the Bank of England thought British industry would need a cash injection of £3,000 million to keep going. In October the *Economist* put the figure at £5,000 million.

News from other countries is much the same. In Germany, a very important bank, Herstatt Bank of Cologne, collapsed with unhonoured debts of more than 1,200 million marks (around £200 million). In the United States, Pan-American Airways is trying, unsuccessfully at the time of writing, to persuade the government to lend it $10.2 million a month to stave off 'imminent financial collapse'. In Japan, Sakamoto Spinning, the Osaka textile firm, went bust in the country's second largest bankruptcy since the war. One thousand Japanese firms collapsed in August alone.

The crisis is becoming more and more a political one. Ruling-class politicians are rattled and scared. On the eve of the October general election, *The Times,* the 'top people's paper', declared that the election would produce a 'last chance parliament'. If it did not find some way to end inflation, 'democracy will be endangered'. Denis Healey stated that unless inflation were checked 'the political and social strains may be too violent for the fabric of our democratic institutions'.

The Conservative Party's election manifesto stated: 'No major democracy has ever survived such a catastrophic rise in the cost of living (20 per cent in a year). We cannot be sure that we would survive.'

The same warning comes from abroad. 'I only have to go to the years 1931 to 1933 [which brought Hitler to power] to say that the meaning of stability is not limited to prices', says West Germany's Chancellor Helmut Schmidt. Michel Debré, who has been both Finance Minister and Prime Minister of France, says: 'Current rates of inflation could be the death blow to democracy and to the future of our Western World.'

The leaders of the establishment are terrified. After a whole generation of full or near-full employment, they find themselves facing unemployment plus inflation plus balance of payments troubles plus low investment – all the afflictions together. And they find that their pundits can't explain anything. Twenty-two economics experts were employed by the government in 1964, and 307 in 1974. Yet the business editor of the *Sunday Times* has to admit: 'the most notable casualty of the period we have just lived through is the notion that we know what we are doing when it comes to running our economic affairs' (29 September 1974).

The disarray among the economics experts is farcical:

When Denis Healey became Chancellor of the Exchequer last March he cast around for a little independent advice. Seven of Britain's best-known economists – top scorers in *The Times'* letters column – were invited to Great George Street to give their thoughts on that most persistent of problems – inflation. On arrival, they immediately fell to squabbling.

Matters were not helped when one of their number said he was having trouble with his model of the British economy and, at that moment, could not say whether the Chancellor should take £1,000 million of spending power out of the economy or pump £1,000 million back in. Mr Healey's brows beetled, he had a Budget to produce in just three weeks.

That skirmish in Mr Healey's office is being repeated in Treasuries, central banks, universities and economic institutes throughout the Western world. Economist lashes at economist as the prairie fire of inflation burns steadily higher and hotter. The cause and the cure for the rapid rise in prices that has swept the Western industrialized countries in the last two years have left economists more divided than ever before.

(Anthony Bambridge, economics editor, *Observer,* 22 September 1974)

The most serious crisis since the 1930s and the pundits of capitalism have no idea where to go. They are split and so are the politicians.

But if they can't agree about the causes, they are sure about the cure. Labour, Liberal and Tory leaders all agree that wages have to be held down one way or another. They only differ about how to do it. The Liberals are for statutory incomes policy; the Tories are for voluntary incomes policy backed by statutory powers; the Labour Party is for the 'social contract' – a voluntary incomes policy.

In the wings there are others – politicians like Enoch Powell or Keith Joseph, or thinking heads like the editor of *The Times* – who preach monetary restraint, a sharp rise in unemployment, as a way to cut down wage claims. Others – still only a handful of right-wingers – recommend the use of private armies or scabs' organizations to do the same thing (Geoffrey Rippon, General Walker, Colonel Stirling). Yet others, like Brigadier Frank Kitson, Commandant, Headquarter School of Infantry, have been proposing for some time that the army be trained for counter-insurgency and strike-breaking functions. Lastly, there is a small group of fascists, the National Front, who are hoping to direct the anxieties of the little man in the street against black people by calling for 'the compulsory repatriation of black immigrants and their offspring'. In this way they hope to get workers to fight among themselves, not against their employers.

In this book we deal with the economic and political issues that the crisis is posing for working-class people – the challenge and the response necessary to overcome the crisis in their interests. Since not many people will want to read the book right through at one go, it is useful to start with a short summary.

The book starts (Chapter One) with an analysis of the present capitalist crisis. This seeks to cut through the gibberish and the pseudo-scientific, financial jargon used by the 'experts'. The chapter is written simply, and factually, so that socialists and militants will be able to grasp the nature of the crisis clearly. Even so a little perseverance will be demanded of the readers for this chapter as well as for Chapter Two.

Chapter Two looks at incomes policy, and shows that it is really a policy for wage restraint in the interests of better profits, for under capitalism profits cannot be controlled for any length of time.

Chapter Three deals with the recent history of incomes policies, starting with Wilson's voluntary policy, of 1965-66, to the compulsory incomes policy of 1966-69 and its collapse after the rebellion of the lower paid. It goes on to the resurrection of a new incomes policy by Ted Heath, once his flirtation with 'Selsdon Man' fell apart after the bankruptcy of Rolls Royce, and the massive unemployment and inflation of winter 1971-72. It then deals with the 'social contract' and threshold agreements – the current methods of holding down wages. A militant programme of demands is counterposed to the 'social contract'.

Chapter Four deals with the other prong of the attack on workers' standards – the use of unemployment. It weighs up the strengths and weaknesses of factory occupations as a reply to sackings, shows how to develop this method of struggle and discusses a general policy against unemployment.

Chapter Five deals with another form of attack on the

workers' real standard of living — cuts in the social services.

In Chapter Six we show how sections of the capitalist class are lurching to the extreme right and toying with the idea of using the law, the police, the army, and private armies, to break strikes and put the workers 'in their place'.

In the next chapter, Chapter Seven, we see what the trade union leaders are doing. Now, more than ever before, there is a struggle inside the unions as well as between the unions and the employers. For the union officials are becoming less and less the *leaders* of the workers, and more and more their foremen.

Chapter Eight deals with the need for workers to build links between different factories and industries, and between different jobs — blue-collar and white-collar. It stresses the need for independent rank and file organization in the trade unions, and warns of the problems that will be met with in building it.

Chapter Nine deals with the crisis of political leadership in the working-class movement, the need to give political content to workers' struggle, to merge the day-to-day struggle against the employers with the struggle against the capitalist system as a whole.

The last chapter is more general. It presents an alternative to the crisis-ridden capitalist system, with its exploitation, anarchy and waste — a system of production for use, planned under workers' control.

We hope this book will prove useful. Today, as always, we need to study the changes that are taking place in capitalism and in the working class; we need to win support amongst other workers for the struggle for socialism; and we need to organize for that struggle. If this book can help at all in these three areas it will have served its purpose.

1.
The Crisis of British Capitalism

The economic crisis in Britain is part of a worldwide crisis in capitalism, a crisis so deep that no country can escape it. Behind it lie important changes that have occurred recently in the structure of the world economy.

The changing pattern of investment

One of the most important changes has been the fantastic growth in size of the big companies. National markets are more and more dominated by a few huge multinational concerns.

Their investments are enormous, both in size and in the time they take to mature. Take cars. In 1970, British Leyland planned to invest £400 million between 1974 and 1978. Volkswagen was expected to invest £1,300 million over the same period, and Fiat at least £750 million. The American giants, General Motors and Ford, and the fast-growing Japanese companies, Nissan and Toyota, all invest as much in a year as British Leyland planned to do in five (Counter Information Services, *British Leyland. The Beginning of the End?* London, 1973, pp. 4-5).

The size of investment in other industries is even greater. I B M, for example, spent $5,000 million developing its 360 series of computers (C. Tugendhat, *The Multinationals*, Pelican, 1971, pp. 82-86).

Like all investment in the past, these huge sums have to come from the workers. But today, as more and more money needs to be spent on investment in plant and machinery compared with wages, it becomes more and more difficult for the capitalist to extract from workers the minimum sums that are necessary. Squeeze as he might,

14

what the capitalist gets out of the workers as surplus is a smaller and smaller amount compared with the constantly growing size of his total investment — his rate of profit falls.

The decline in the rate of profit

That the squeeze has been increasing is very clear. A careful analysis of the rate of exploitation in Britain concludes that it has doubled in the last 100 years, and it is rising faster now than ever before (Lionel Sims, unpublished article submitted to *International Socialism*).

It is also true that many important companies have made very large profits recently: I C I's pre-tax profit in the first six months of 1974 was £254 million compared with £137 million in the first half of last year, a rise of 71 per cent. Shell's first quarter profit this year — £319 million — was up three times on the same period in 1973. British Petroleum made £295½ million, Unilever £90.7 million. Other increases over the year included: Reed International 74 per cent, Courtaulds 71 per cent, Cadbury-Schweppes 95 per cent. Overall, pre-tax profits of industrial companies rose 44.4 per cent between the first half of 1973 and 1974 — quite a hefty rise (*Sunday Times,* 21 July 1974).

Throughout the last dozen years, total company profits have shown a general trend upwards, as can be seen from the following table:

Gross UK trading profits of companies
(in £ million)

1962	3,595	1968	5,275
1963	4,103	1969	5,159
1964	4,544	1970	5,159
1965	4,741	1971	5,761
1966	4,610	1972	6,666
1967	4,663	1973	8,632

From: Central Statistical Office, *National Income and Expenditure 1973,* London, 1973, p.32.

But while the *amount* of profit has been rising, the *rate* of profit has been showing a clear tendency downward..In the last 25 years pre-tax profits for large companies have almost halved:

Pre-tax rate of profit of quoted companies in manufacturing, construction, communication and distribution

1950-54	16.5 per cent
1955-59	14.7 per cent
1960-64	13.0 per cent
1965-69	11.7 per cent
1970-	9.7 per cent

From: Glyn and B. Sutcliffe, *British Capitalism, Workers and the Profits Squeeze,* London 1972, p.66.

The decline has been particularly steep since the mid-fifties.

Rate of profit (before tax) on capital in the company sector 1955-71

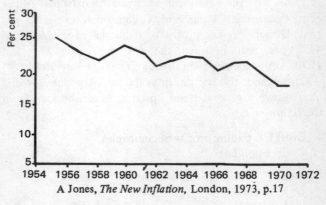

A Jones, *The New Inflation,* London, 1973, p.17

Rapacious banks take their pound of flesh

The decline in profit rates in industry has not stopped the banks from increasing theirs.

One result of the growth of multinational companies was

the formation in the 1960s of a worldwide currency and capital market in which billions of pounds worth of currency were able to rush from one financial centre to another. In order to keep funds from stampeding, each government pushed up interest rates. In Britain, Bank Rate or the official minimum lending rate climbed inexorably upwards from 2 per cent in 1945-49 to 12½ per cent on 11 April 1974.

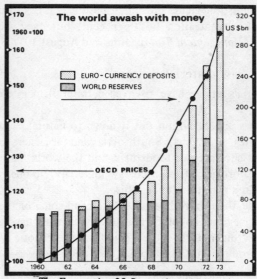

The Economist, 28 September 1974

Banks charge their commercial and industrial customers more than that, so, as these customers were forced by their declining profit rates to seek bank finance, profits in banking and finance shot far ahead. Between 1964 and 1973 the after-tax profit of some of the banks rose as follows:

Barclays	886 per cent
Lloyds	1,042 per cent
Midlands	687 per cent
Kayser Ulman	3,998 per cent

Finance companies' profits rose even more fantastically:

Slater Walker	16,990 per cent
Trafalgar House (8 years)	5,969 per cent
First National Finance	3,442 per cent

As against this, the profits of industrial companies rose much less: G K N 116 per cent, E M I 200 per cent, Unilever 166, Hoover 165, Plessey 113, Metal Box 93, Dunlop 153, British Leyland 35.

Some industrial giants did much better: G E C 918 per cent, Rank Organization 662 per cent; but they were exceptions (*Management Today*, June and August 1974).

Rise in raw materials prices

Raw materials prices have risen even faster than interest rates. Why?

The press and television put it down to natural causes. Crop failures in Russia, South Asia and elsewhere are blamed for shortages of foodstuffs, and the world 'energy crisis' for shortages of essential raw materials. No-one, we are told, can do anything about this.

It is true there have been shortages and some of them have been beyond anyone's control. But many have resulted not from natural causes, but from the chaotic way capitalist production is organized. Take food:

The present crisis really seems to have got under way just over two years ago when the whole balance of the world market in grain changed.

Until then, the Western capitalist countries had unchallenged sway over the world market. There were big surpluses. Farmers in the United States were even paid not to grow crops.

Meanwhile millions of hungry people, unable to make their demand effective as they had no money, were left to starve. It was unthinkable that surpluses should be given away. Far more important that prices be kept up and profit levels guaranteed.

But the balance of the market was changing. Japan and Russia began to buy on the market. No longer did one single bloc of countries dominate.

This coincided with several disastrous harvests which called forth a familiar response from the profit-oriented market economy. Feed the hungry? No, jack up prices.

(L. Flynn, 'Enough to Turn Your Stomach,' *Socialist Worker*, 28 September 1974)

'Destroy wheat' farmers told

In a move to slash a record wheat surplus, the Canadian Federal Government today offered the country's Western farmers 100 million dollars (£39 million) or more to destroy most of the 1970 crop.

The emergency programme was described in Ottawa by Mr Otto Lang, minister responsible for wheat, as an initiative which should help international efforts to stabilise the grain economy.

—Press Association report

Or take the case of oil. In 1971-72 the big US oil companies deliberately held back production, so as to force price increases from the government and to drive smaller independent oil-marketing companies out of business. By 1973 supplies were short and the United States began to buy oil from the Arab states. The increased demand for Arab oil allowed the producers, including the same oil companies who held back US production in the first place, to push up prices.

Or take chemicals. In Europe in 1970-72 the big chemical combines decided that their profits were not high enough to justify expansion on the lines they had planned earlier. So when industrial output grew at an unexpected rate last year, there were just not enough chemical products to go round, and their prices shot up.

When prices start rising it makes sense for wealthy people and companies to protect their wealth against inflation and to make a profit by buying up future supplies of food and raw materials. By competing for these supplies they push prices up even further.

No wonder City investment advisers Sausmarez, Carey and Harris told their clients: 'In view of the world shortage of raw materials, we feel there is a case for investing a slice of an investor's portfolio in these markets ... The right decision can put equities growth in the shade.'

The result is that as much as 30-75 per cent of the increases in prices of food and raw materials have not resulted from shortages at all, but from speculation (*Guardian*, 13 February 1974).

That speculators in raw materials had a marvellous time, although some of them, like Rowntree, miscalculated, can be seen from the fantastic gap between market prices and production costs.

Relationships between long-run production costs and world market prices

	Estimated costs	Approx. price	Price as % of costs
Rubber (p/kilo)	20	35	180
Tin (£/ton)	1,750	4,000	230
Sugar cane (£/ton)	90	230	260
Zinc (£/ton)	300	870	290
Copper (£/ton)	450	1,350	300
Cocoa (£/ton)	300	1,000	330
Oil (OPEC) cents/barrel	20	800	4,000

From: *The Economist,* London, 11-17 May 1974, pp. 76-77.

The really big beneficiaries of rising commodity prices are the giant Western companies which control production and marketing internationally: Anglo-American (profits up 35 per cent in 1973), Rio Tinto Zinc (profits nearly double), the oil companies which, in the United States alone, expect an extra $13,000 million a year as a result of the rise in oil prices at home and abroad.

Price policy in the giant industrial company

Forty or fifty years ago, companies cut prices with every economic downturn. Now they don't. The giants dominating the major industries now arrive at their prices by 'cost-plus' calculations. A rise in the interest they have to pay or the price of raw materials they buy is simply passed on in higher prices for their finished goods. A decline in their output which raises overhead costs per unit also raises their prices. Even a decline in profits raises prices: not only does the giant company try to compensate itself for narrowing profit margins, but it creates more and more unused industrial capacity, more and more overhead and distribution costs, in order to beat the competition.

There is an impeccable witness to argue big business' inflationary crimes – none other than the Joint Economic Committee of the United States Congress. The current inflation, they say, cannot be blamed on either of the traditional 'causes' – excess demand or union excesses. Nor can crop failures, dollar devaluation, the oil-cost explosion, or any other special factor expain the extent of recent increases. They go on to state:

> Increasingly, a significant part of the current inflation can be explained only in the context of administered prices in concentrated industries. They typically increase despite falling demand, at the same time as structural distortions in both government and business are stifling competition and efficiency.
>
> (Reported in *Financial Times,* 3 October 1974)

Big business knows how to make prices go up, better than it knows how to bring them down. Take this report as an example:

> the price of nearly every key raw material has fallen back in recent months to 1972 levels, but prices in the shops are as high

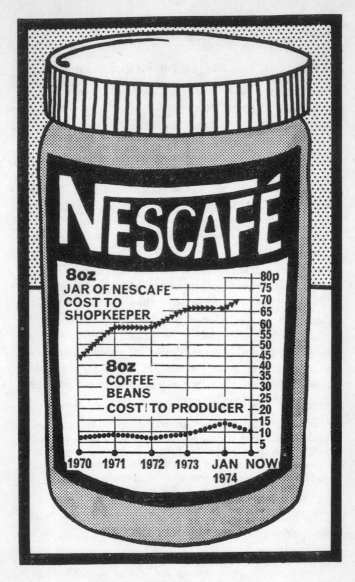

From: *The Observer*, 6 October 1974

as ever . . . the base metals should all be costing industry significantly less than at the time of the last general election. One vital
metal, copper, used in housebuilding and construction, shipbuilding and electronics, is being sold for half the price it fetched
in February. . .

The same is true of goods that affect weekly household budgets.
This week has seen further falls in the price of wool and rubber,
while coffee bought on the world market today would be 20p a
pound, 4½p less than at the start of this year.

Yet *The Grocer* noted 466 food price rises this week . . .

Coffee provides an interesting example. . . The packaged product
is sold to the trade at a price of about £1.50 a pound, compared
with £1.30 at the start of this year, and £1.16 a pound in 1971.
This represents a mark-up for the manufacturing process profit
of about 500 per cent on the cost of beans at the high prices
prevailing at the start of this year.

The fall in bean costs brings the mark-up to 650 per cent, but
manufacturers have not reduced the trade price . . . .

(Colin Chapman, *Observer,* 6 October 1974)

Government spending

The growth of government has been as spectacular and as
important as the growth of the multinational company.
And government taxation and spending policies have become major independent sources of inflation as a result.

Over the last 20 years more and more taxes have come
out of working-class incomes and less and less from big
business:

	1949-52	1965-68
Percentage of wages taken by tax	9.8	15.5
Percentage of corporate profits (inc. dividends) taken by tax	45.6	30.9

From: D. Jackson, H.A. Turner and F. Wilkinson, *Do
Trade Unions Cause Inflation?* Cambridge, 1972, p.80.

To make good the loss, workers have had to push for

wage increases which have then been passed on by business in higher prices. For this reason, the government often feels it dare not increase taxation. Instead, it finances its expenditure by printing money. The money supply rises faster than the quantity of goods in the shops, and prices rise. In 1973 money supply rose 30 per cent.

To get some idea of what the government spends its money on look at state expenditure in 1972:

The Military Budget (aim: to defend capitalists against external enemies) — total spending £3,059 million.

Trade and Industry Budget (aim: to provide finance and assistance to the private sector of the economy) — total spending £1,615 million (up by 25 per cent in 12 months).

Nationalized Industry Investment (aim: to build up sections of the economy for the benefit of private capital where private capital does not find it profitable enough to invest itself) — total spending £1,660 million.

Law and Order (aim: to protect private industrial wealth against those who made it and might appropriate it) — total spending £764 million.

Motorways (aim: to provide private industrial concerns with easy transport to markets) — total spending £297 million.

National Debt Interest (aim: to pay capitalists interest on loans they made to the state to fight their wars) — total spending £1,599 million.

By contrast:

Social Security Supplementary Benefits — total spending £641 million.

Family Allowances — total spending £343 million.

Direct government aid to industry has been enormous. Anthony Wedgwood Benn found 'no fewer than 16 separate financial assistance schemes in existence, including regional development, investment support, general assistance, aerospace, shipbuilding, tourism and research and development'. In the four years from April 1970 'government returned to industry about half the taxation industry paid to government. Or put in another way, government has been financing just under half the payment of dividends to shareholders' (*Financial Times*, 6 May 1974).

In the long run this kind of aid can only add to the inflationary pressure, and deepen the capitalist crisis as a whole. For the companies that receive the aid are helped because they are big, not because they are efficient or competitive.

Milking the nationalized industries for the private sector

In the mid-fifties, something like £70 million a year was transferred from the nationalized industries to the private sector by means of artificially low prices. By the end of the fifties the annual sum was more like £100 million a year (John Hughes, 'Relations with Private Industry', in M. Shanks (ed.), *Lessons of Public Enterprise*, 1963, p. 128). The cost of that transfer in taxes was estimated by the Select Committee on Nationalized Industries (1968) at £90 million a year for every 1 per cent decline in earning power imposed on the public sector (*Ministerial Control of the Nationalized Industries*, vol. 2, p. 1).

The nationalized industries are still being milked. To take one example: the British Steel Corporation, in evidence to the Commons Select Committee on Nationalized Industries, published in April 1973, claims that the disallowed price increases it requested reached nearly £400 million.

In 20 years to 1968 the public sector grew at 3.4 per cent a year as against 2.8 per cent in private manufacturing. In the latter half of this period the publicly-owned industries were doing even better – 5.3 per cent as against 3.7

per cent (Richard Pryke, quoted in *Guardian*, 25 September 1974).

The fact that in spite of this success nationalized industries needed to get massive subsidies — £1,843 million from 1968 to 1973 — shows how ruthlessly they have been milked.

These subsidies are inflationary. They raise the money supply without increasing the amount of goods available.

Oil fuels stagflation

Last winter's fantastic fourfold rise in the price of oil, and in the income of the oil countries' ruling class, could have catastrophic consequences for Western capitalism. To the extent the oil exporters use their new income to buy goods here, prices rise because of the increased price of their oil and because of the loss of goods in payment for it. To the extent they keep their new income here, prices rise because of the high interest rates needed to persuade them to do so. To the extent that the economic crisis has made them nervous about locking up their money on a large scale for any length of time, they are adding to the general instability of the system and placing immense strains on the world's banking and financial systems. In the words of one report:

> Banks as large as the Chase Manhattan in New York have given warning that sooner or later the problem of trying to cope with short-term borrowing and long-term loans, as well as financing not so much commercial enterprises, but whole national economies, will prove too much for the banks. Some have already gone under as a result of the stresses and strains set up in the financial system. Before long the whole banking structure could come tumbling down.

(John Palmer, *Guardian*, 9 October 1974)

In Britain the amount of hot oil money is rising very quickly. The same report states:

The holdings of oil-exporting states in Britain amounted to £6,967 million at the end of June, a growth of 115.9 per cent over the end-1973 position of £3,227 million.

Wages

If wages did not chase prices, inflatory pressure would be lessened. But, seeing that labour costs are only *one* factor in the inflationary spiral, even static money wages would not stop the rise in prices – last year, according to the *Economist*, they would still have risen by 7.4 per cent even if wages had stood still.

It is possible to see from the following table that wages have not been the main cause of price rises in Britain in 1973. Britain, which comes bottom of the wage rise league, comes top in food price rises and third from top in all price rises (the figures are given in percentages):

Wages		Food prices		All prices	
Italy	28.5	Britain	19	Italy	11
Denmark	20	Denmark	15.5	Denmark	11
Belgium	15.5	Italy	11.5	Britain	10
France	14	France	10.5	France	8
Holland	13	Germany	7	Holland	8
Britain	12	Holland	7	Germany	7

From: *The Economist,* 9 February 1974

We have already shown that taxation is behind much of the inflationary wage-push. Together with rising prices it forces workers to fight for wage rises. The stronger organized labour is, the more effectively does it defend itself against the price rises engineered by big business and big government.

Socialist Worker, 25 November 1972

Weakening the springs of growth

Why now? Why did all the factors mentioned in this chapter not cause a crisis ten, or five, years ago? The reason lies in the run-down of what is known as the Permanent Arms Economy.

Since 1940 a larger portion of the surplus value produced by workers has been used for war or war preparations than ever before in the history of capitalism (except for the years 1914-18). In the United States as much was spent on arms in the fifties as on industrial investment; in Britain today more goes on arms than on investment in manufacturing industry.

This meant that a sizeable proportion of the surplus available for investment was no longer subject to the fluctuating fortunes of boom and slump. Industry grew much more evenly than in the past.

This set-up could not continue for ever: the economies of Japan and Germany and Italy, not burdened with arms spending, were able to grow much more rapidly than those of the United States or Britain. The US arms economy provided them with a market for their goods, while they themselves devoted all their resources to expanding production, not arms. The US economy grew at 3 or 4 per cent a year throughout the 1950s and 1960s; the European economies at 5-6 per cent; the Japanese economy between 10 and 15 per cent.

One result was that the United States came under increasing pressure to cut the proportion of its own national income devoted to arms. All told, the proportion of Western resources spent on arms fell from 7.5 per cent in 1955 to 4 per cent in 1965 and has continued to fall since.

The decline in arms spending has meant a decline in its stabilizing effect, as has been shown graphically over the last few years, first with the simultaneous Western boom of the late 1960s and now with the world recession.

The decline in arms spending has pushed us into a world recession. But its continued high level ensures that the scale of unemployment and decline in production will be less than in the recessions at the end of the nineteenth century and during the twenties and thirties of the present century. This time, however, because capitalism has changed in structure, recession is accompanied by inflation.

In all probability world production will start rising again in 1976. But there is no comfort in that for the system. For, as the editor of *The Times* writes, in a spasm of paralytic terror:

Taking the free world as a whole, the depression is likely to be sufficiently severe and the amount of money required to counteract it sufficiently large – larger than ever before – that a vast further addition to the world money supply will be created in 1975. This will put the world economy back into boom conditions in the second half of the four year cycle, that is in 1976 and 1977, but it will do so at the expense of a world inflation almost certainly much greater than the inflationary peak of 1973 and early 1974 ... At the end of the next boom, it can be expected that the financial structure of major countries will break down, and that the financial calamity which we have probably narrowly avoided in the last boom will really hit us.

(26 September 1974)

In conclusion

The combination of inflation and stagnation, the fact that when output goes down prices do not follow, but on the contrary go up, is because both big business and the workers are well organized; the first in the multinationals and in government, the second in the trade unions. Big business' strong organization enables it to push prices upwards whenever costs go up. The workers' organization allows them to push wages up in an effort to keep level with rising prices.

So the central core of stagflation is the war of attrition between organized capital and organized labour. Repeatedly efforts are made by one side or the other to go on the offensive and break the stalemate. Heath's aggressive policy of confrontation smashed the postmen in 1971. But in 1972 he was beaten — by the miners on the wages front, and by the dockers on the political front (remember the Pentonville Five and the Industrial Relations Act). Then, in 1973 Ted Heath won the battles of Phases One, Two, and Three, at the expense of local government workers, teachers, hospital ancillary workers, and even engineers. But finally, in 1974, he was beaten industrially and politically by the miners.

Socialist Worker, 6 October 1973

2.
Incomes Policy or Wages Policy?

Labour, Tory and Liberal leaders all speak of the need for incomes policy. The Liberals are for statutory incomes policy, the Tories are at present arguing for a voluntary one but with statutory backing if need be. The Labour Party leaders are committed for the moment to a voluntary incomes policy – the 'social contract'.

What do these politicians mean by incomes policy? Is it anything more than a policy to restrain wages?

When Labour introduced its first incomes policy in 1965, it stressed that the aim of the operation was not to control wages alone. It was 'not just a wages policy but an incomes policy ... not only just an incomes policy but a prices and incomes policy' (George Brown to the Conference of Executives of Trade Unions on 30 April 1965). The government was at pains to argue that the incomes policy would be perfectly fair because it would apply equally to all incomes. In this chapter we shall discuss whether there is any truth in this claim.

Can profits be controlled?

There is a qualitative difference between wages and profits: wages are a necessary part of the costs of production while profits are not; profits are what is left over after production and sale, while wages are not; wages are negotiated between two sides, while profits are not. It is nonsense to talk of putting the same restraints on profits and wages since profits cannot be planned.

Profits, moreover, are the motor of capitalism and its only reliable guide to how well an enterprise is doing. Michael Spicer put the argument clearly:

It is precisely because profits *do* play a specific and essential role in the capitalist economy – in providing the finance for expansion, the inducement to invest and the stimulus to efficiency – that their control is such a hazardous, not to say impossible, operation.

So long . . . as we maintain the capitalist rules of the game, so long as we continue to discard the idea of a total state planning, we must allow profits a high degree of flexibility.

('Implementing an Incomes Policy, 3 – And What About Profits?' *The Statist,* 8 January 1965)

The same point was made by the management of the Dunlop Rubber Company, when they published *Dunlop's Statement of Intent* in support of George Brown's:

Profits for Security and Growth. We are in a competitive business. Our success is measured by the profits we make. Augment them, be proud of them and recognize them as the fund which provides our security and the tools for our future success.

And Professor Paish put the argument against a profit-freeze under capitalism in a nutshell:

To try and peg profits would mean that every firm would be working on a cost-plus basis and would lose all incentive to keep down costs.

(F. W. Paish, *The Limits of Incomes Policies,* London, Institute of Economic Affairs, 1964, p. 20)

No: profit is the life-blood of capitalism. If you are allergic to profit then you just can't run a capitalist economy. Therefore, as long as the Labour leaders are committed to such an economy they cannot and dare not harm, or gag, profits. A Fabian writer, J. R. Sargent, was really quite consistent when he argued that a Labour government should allow a *more unequal* distribution of income, in the interests of capital accumulation and a faster rate of growth. As he pointed out, if wages rose seriously compared with profits, the effect could be quite disastrous:

As the share of wages continued to rise, and profit margins were further eroded, the life-blood of capitalism would begin to run dry. Capital would try to flee abroad, and would presumably be checked by applying exchange control with the necessary severity. This done, businesses would gradually begin to close down, as there would be insufficient profit to induce them to replace their worn-out assets.

(J. R. Sargent, *Out of Stagnation,* London, 1963, p. 33)

Denis Healey drew the same conclusion when he spoke to the Confederation of British Industries at its annual dinner in May 1974:

The investor must be satisfied that he will receive an adequate return on the capital he invests, and this return must be judged against the prospects for inflation. I know we may not always agree on what constitutes a sufficient return, but at least nobody now believes that profit is a dirty word, if profit is honestly earned and put to proper social use.

(*Financial Times,* 15 May 1974)

Price control

Profits are what is left from the sale price of a commodity after its costs of production have been deducted. So, to control profits, there must also be control of prices. In fact, price control is an extremely complicated, indeed an impossible task.

First of all, price formation is a very intricate process:

Price leadership, marginal selling, optimum product and price 'mixes', branding, scale economies, the concept of 'the contribution', and pioneer profit ideas are just a few among literally dozens of subtleties which can make price figuring among the most complicated arithmetic business gets involved in.

(Christopher George, 'Snags for Industry in a Prices Review', *The Statist,* 1 January 1965)

The number of price changes is fantastically large. The Department of Economic Affairs estimated that something like three million prices are altered each year, that is 2,000 for each of the 250 members of the Price Commission staff. These poor people have to evaluate all the price increases requested, check the quarterly returns, make spot checks on a myriad of small firms, and make sure that all the figures they are given are valid, even though they have nothing better than unaudited accounts to deal with, or, alternatively, year-old audited ones. And if they do get anywhere, the maximum fine that can be imposed for illegal price increases is £400 – what a deterrent!

The rules for fixing prices are full of loopholes. First, there are the exceptions which cover a large proportion of expenditure:

- exports and imports (on first sale);
- fresh food, from the producers;
- goods on a commodity market, or prices determined by reference to it (eg. London Metal Exchange);
- internationally determined prices, such as for coal and steel;
- drugs supplied to the N H S and defence purchases;
- auctioned items, secondhand goods (except cars), interest charges;
- insurance (which is under the D T I), etc.

Second, where the rules do apply, they are highly involved. In practice, very little price monitoring actually takes place. In the first five months of Phase Three, the Price Commission rejected 705 price increases and modified 240. Some of these modifications were extremely small. For example, in March 1974 a 79.4 per cent claim from Monsanto was modified by 0.02 per cent; a 14.8 per cent claim from Goodyear was modified by 0.003 per cent.

During the whole period of Phases One, Two and the first five months of Phase Three, only one company had to defy a Commission order to reduce prices – there were no others, which is not surprising since price increases of up to 80 per cent were being allowed through. Some requests for increases were 'withdrawn': I C I, for example, withdrew a request for a 118 per cent increase in the price of acetone, which suggests that it was a try-on in the first place. The Racecourse Association withdrew a request for a 16.6 per cent price increase for 'commentaries on races' broadcast through betting shops. *Every month* by contrast, *The Grocer* notifies between 500 and 600 major price increases in groceries alone.

What more is there to say? The *Economist* accurately saw the role of the Price Commission as one of arranging the least damaging sorts of cosmetics. And that is precisely what the Tories used it for. In December 1972 they declared: 'So far so good. The government's 90-day stand-still on prices, pay, rents and dividends is now in force. It gives Britain the biggest chance yet to break the vicious spiral of inflation' (*Conservative Monthly News,* December 1972). Then in April 1973: 'The great battle to break the back of inflation enters a fresh stage this month' (*Conservative Monthly News,* April 1973). Again in October 1973: 'We are now applying a strict and effective pattern for the control of prices' (Sir Geoffrey Howe, Minister for Trade and Consumer Affairs, 17 October 1973, House of Commons).

Socialist Worker, 6 April 1974

The 'profit equals dividends' trick

One way of selling an incomes policy to the labour movement is by pretending that dividends and profits are the same thing, or that dividends make up a decisive proportion of profits. It is not uncommon today for apologists of incomes policy within the labour movement to present the control of dividends as a fair bargain for the control of wages.

Wages are the only payment that workers get for the sale of their labour-power; but dividends *are not* the only payment that capitalists get for the ownership of capital. The dividend is only part of the payment to the shareholder. If a worker gets a wage rise of £1.50 a week instead of £2, the extra 50p are never kept for him to draw at a later date. What a worker loses in wages now is never seen again. But with a shareholder it is different. If he gets a dividend of £1.50 out of a profit of £2, the other 50p are invested on his behalf and come back to him later as a capital gain on his share of the company. What the shareholder loses in dividends now he *does* see again, in another form.

It is a central feature of the contemporary tax scene that the capitalist *prefers* capital gains to dividend income. Freezing dividends does not suppress capital gains; it makes them even bigger. In fact, it has been calculated that over the years capital gain has on average been equal to the total amount of dividends distributed, and that it went up 4.7 per cent per year on average between 1919 and 1968, or 2.7 per cent per year in real terms (A. B. Atkinson, *Unequal Shares, Wealth in Britain,* Penguin, 1974, p. 35).

Dividends and capital gains are not the only bonuses for the rich:

Directors' fees

A number of companies pay their chairmen £30,000 a year

or more. A selection of them is given here:

Chairman	Company	Salary* £
F. S. McFadzean**	Shell	75,900
P. W. Milligan	Sedgwick Forbes Holdings	68,000
Sir Eric Drake	British Petroleum	66,270
S. W. Wade	Frost & Reed (Holdings)	66,085
E. J. Callard	Imperial Chemical Industries	65,540
Sir Val Duncan	Rio Tinto Zinc Corporation	63,000
Sir John Reiss	Associated Portland Cement Manufacturers	59,183
W. Emmott	Automotive Products Associated	58,272
Sir John Davis	Rank Organization	55,000
Sir Halford Reddish	Rugby Portland Cement	50,806
Lord Stokes	British Leyland Motor	48,560
Sir William Batty**	Ford Motor Company	47,400
Sir Raymond Brookes	Guest Keen & Nettlefolds	47,000
E. G. Woodroofe	Unilever	47,000
Sir Brian Mountain	Eagle Star Insurance	45,000
Sir Arnold Hall	Hawker Siddeley Group	42,872

*   Year ending on 31.12.72 in every case except British Leyland and Rank Organization whose years ended on 30.9.72 and 31.10.72.

**   Appointed during the year. Annual rate of salary, not the amount actually received.

From: Labour Research Department, *Two Nations,* London 1973, p.12.

In addition we should not forget the man that gets the top director's salary in the country: R. Tompkins of Green Shield Stamps. His salary is £288,834 a year.

Some of these directors have had quite large pay rises to keep up with the dreadful rise in prices. In 1973, Sir John Davis got a rise of £10,000; Sir Val Duncan a rise of £6,000; Ernest Woodroofe, a rise of £3,069. A. J. McAlpine's salary was raised by 62 per cent from a mere £41,565; Sir John Clark's salary was raised by 35.8 per cent, from £48,000; and Sir John Spencer Wills, a rise of a mere 10.5 per cent, from £51,400.

Many of these directors sit on the boards of a number of companies, and receive fees for doing so. Sir John Davis has 16 other directorships including Eagle Star and Southern Television (of which he is chairman); Sir Brian Mountain is a director of 44 companies and chairman of 20 of them.

Golden handshakes

Here are a few examples. Sir John Cockfield resigned as managing director of Boots in 1966 with a golden hand-shake of £55,000. (Some time later Sir John became chairman of the Price Commission.) Martin Trowbridge, resigning as director of Pegler Hattersley after ten months, received £40,000 (*Financial Times,* 5 July 1973). Ronald Plumley resigned as chairman of Venesta International and received £42,000 (*Financial Times,* 4 July 1973). Sir John Wall, chairman of International Computers since 1968, received £56,000 as compensation for loss of office (*Financial Times,* 3 January 1973). And Mr Aubrey Jones, who became non-executive chairman of Laporte Industries at £20,000 a year when he retired from the Prices and Incomes Board in November 1970, was paid compensation of £63,000 in August 1972 when he left Laporte. The Lonrho affair provided an even more startling example, when it was revealed that Mr Duncan Sandys had been offered £130,000 to terminate the consultancy for which he had been paid an annual fee of £51,000. The con-sultancy started in November 1971, on the 'mutual under-standing', according to the managing director Mr Rowland, that it was to have been for six years. When it was terminated in March 1972, Mr Sandys agreed to become part-time chairman of Lonrho at £38,000 a year.

Fat pensions and perks

It takes 40 years for an ordinary person to be entitled to

the maximum pension rate, but for the 'top hats' ten years is enough. In their case, pensions reach two-thirds of their salary before retirement.

> The managing director of a large company who gets a salary of £20,000 a year can look forward to a pension of £13,333 a year or £256 a week; or alternatively to one of £10,000 a year and a tax-free lump sum of £30,000.
>
> Companies are not required to reveal the amount of the contributions they make towards their directors' pensions, so naturally very few of them do. A few companies, however, state the total pension contribution made for all their directors. Thus C. T. Bowring and Co (insurance, banking, etc.) paid £119,000 in pension contributions in 1972 for its 15 directors, an average of £8,000 each, or nearly a third of their total pay. And the Plessey Company paid £56,000 in 1972 for its 12 directors, an average of £4,666 per director. Since these are averages, the payments for the more highly paid directors must be a good deal higher; they are seldom revealed, but the *Financial Times* of 18.1.67 reported that the contribution towards the pension of the chairman of the National Provincial Bank was £12,766 a year. I C I paid out in 1972 a staggering £748,000 in directors' pension contributions and in pensions and gratuities to former directors.
>
> In contrast, the annual contribution made by a company with a good pension scheme for its manual workers is not likely to exceed £200 per head, and will often be much less.
>
> (Labour Research Department, *Two Nations,* pp. 18-19).

In addition generous tax-free expenses and fringe benefits are available to many directors and top executives in great variety: entertainment and travel expenses, company cars, company houses, medical benefits, payment of public school fees.

It has been estimated that expenditure on spirits and imported wines on business account totalled £33 million in 1955. Since then the directors' thirst has increased. Government statisticians estimated that 8 per cent of all wines and spirits consumed in the mid-sixties were on tax-free business account.

This means that in 1972 business entertainment accounted for over £110 million worth of wines and spirits. An example of this sort of living was revealed during the Briant Colour Printing work-in, when the joint chapels committee discovered, amongst many other things, that the owner of the company had, only days before his company went into liquidation, thrown a champagne party complete with hired marquee, expensive food, etc. to celebrate the opening of his new private swimming pool. The afternoon's jollities were all invoiced to the company.

(Labour Research Department, *Two Nations,* p. 23)

A survey of London night clubs and late-night restaurants showed that most of the bills for entertainment were paid by firms and not by individuals. As the *Economist* put it: 'Only Exchequer largesses paid directly via the tax-free expense account keep the night-club industry ticking at all' (11 April 1959, p. 105, quoted in R. M. Titmuss, *Income Distribution and Social Change,* London: Allen and Unwin, 1963, p. 180).

Tax fiddles

A worker cannot avoid paying taxes. The rich can and do. A large industry has grown up, comprising accountants, tax consultants, lawyers and others, who devote themselves, with the help of insurance companies, banks and other City institutions, to the highly remunerative business of advising the wealthy on the art of tax avoidance.

Michael Meacher, the Labour M P, estimated that on death duties alone the rich cheated by over £700 million a year, or twice as much as the actual tax yield in 1969 (*Tribune,* 15 October 1971).

Between 1908 and 1915 one-fifth of government revenue was derived from estate duties. Over the last few years this tax produced only one twenty-ninth of total revenue (J. C. Kincaid, *Poverty and Equality in Britain,* Penguin, 1973, pp. 110-11). The Inland Revenue estimates that total personal wealth in 1968 was about £88,000 million. Meacher has calculated that the true figure was in the region of £267,000 million, with the difference not subject to any form of tax.

Meacher produced an enlightening comparison of tax evasion at the top of society with welfare benefit fraud at the bottom of society. He writes:

In 1971, 9,033 people were forced to hand over nearly £12 million to the Inland Revenue after proven evasion of tax ... Yet the prosecution rate is about 120 a year, or 11.3 per cent. By contrast, the prosecution rate for benefit fraud, although the sums are much smaller, is 22.5 per cent.

(Counter Information Service, *Three Phase Trick*, London, 1973)

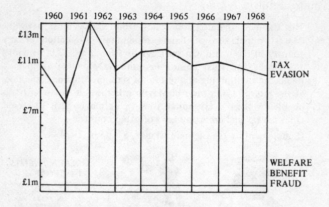

One loophole open to the rich is the so-called tax haven. Remember the Lonrho affair in May 1973, when it was revealed that Mr Rowland, the managing director, had agreed to pay Mr Duncan Sandys, Tory M P and a former Cabinet Minister, a consultancy fee of £51,000 a year for 'U K and overseas services'; and that the overseas fee of £49,000 was to be paid in the Cayman Islands. The May issue of *The Banker,* a monthly magazine owned by the *Financial Times* group, wrote in its annual review of offshore investment centres and tax havens that the Cayman Islands had 'reached the front rank of offshore tax havens'. And the survey concludes: 'The future of offshore financial centres looks very bright indeed.' Other tax havens examined in the survey are the Channel Islands, the Isle of Man, Bermuda, the Bahamas, Hong Kong, Panama, Liberia and, among the promising newcomers, the New Hebrides and Nauru in the Pacific. Using these places for tax avoidance is expensive and 'It's not really worth trying by anyone earning less than £25,000 a year or with less than maybe £500,000 capital', according to an accountant reported in the *Daily Mail,* 19 May 1973.

In case the reader wants to go to the Cayman Islands, this information supplied by the *Financial Times* will be quite useful:

> The Cayman Islands, 200 miles from Cuba, must have the densest population of banks to human population of any country in the world. On the Cayman Islands are 13,000 people, 170 banks and trust companies, and 5,071 other companies. Banks are multiplying at the rate of six a month, and companies at the rate of 120 a month. Maybe it is the climate that attracts people to these West Indian islands, or maybe it is to escape from the tax and company laws of other countries.

(Supplement on the Cayman Islands, 5 August 1974)

GREAT MOMENTS IN CRIME NO. 24.

THE ARREST OF ALBERT PLUCKLEY IN BRAZIL FOR FRAUDULENTLY OBTAINING £1·34 SOCIAL SECURITY MONEY

Socialist Worker, 1 June 1974

In conclusion

When incomes policy is referred to in the press, or television and in parliament, what is almost always meant is a policy for wages.

Even if such an incomes policy ensured that dividends did not rise faster than wages, it could not guarantee that profits as a whole would not rise faster than wages, or that other perks for the capitalist would be covered by the 'equality' of treatment. Even if the rate of growth of wages and profits were equal, it would still be unfair. For the points from which the worker and the capitalist start are quite different. Five per cent added to a weekly wage of £40 is nothing like 5 per cent added to a profit of £1 million.

3.
The Social Contract - A New Form of Incomes Policy

Wilson's incomes policy Mark I

In October 1964 Harold Wilson came to power. In December of that year George Brown, the Secretary of State for Economic Affairs, published a *Statement of Intent on Productivity, Prices and Incomes,* a statement to which both the T U C and the C B I appended their signatures.

To give backing to the incomes policy, an economic plan for expansion was framed. It was published as the *National Plan,* a book of 474 pages, in September 1965.

Harold Wilson and his friends took it for granted that this plan for a smooth expansion of production would be the foundation for the newly adopted incomes policy. As he told the Transport and General Workers' Union in July 1963,

> The Tories' policy is to cut production down (except in election years) and then tailor the wage system to fit it. Our policy is to expand production and relate our national incomes policy to it.
>
> (Quoted in P. Foot, *The Politics of Harold Wilson,* Penguin, 1968, p. 142)

Wilson sold Labour's incomes policy as 'a planned growth of wages'. As such it was accepted by the unions. At the 1961 Labour Party Conference Frank Cousins, then General Secretary of the Transport and General Workers' Union, had stated in a militant speech: 'We are not willing to accept in any form, shape or disguise wage restraint.' He was cheered lustily by the platform, led by Wilson and Gaitskell. A planned *growth* of wages, was, they assured themselves, an entirely different matter.

Two years later, Frank Cousins actually introduced the phrase 'planned growth of incomes' to the Labour Party

Conference. He said:

> We mean we want a planned rate of economic growth which will
> enable us to have improvements in our real standards of wages.

Summing up on behalf of the party's National Executive
James Callaghan said:

> The framework in which we shall try to work out an incomes
> policy is: first, there must be an expanding economy; secondly,
> the government's policy must work in harmony with the policies
> we are asking the trade unions and the employers to follow.
>
> (A. Fisher and B. Dix, *Low Pay and How to End it*, London,
> 1974, p. 19)

If economic planning and the planned growth of wages
were the twin pillars of Wilson's first incomes policy, one of
the main criteria of its success was the benefits that would
accrue to the lower-paid workers. In the words of the
Statement of Intent, the government's objective was 'to
ensure that the benefits of faster growth are distributed in a
way that satisfies the claims of social need and justice.'

If only workers in a stronger position would forgo wage
rises, it would help the lower-paid workers. Or so Harold
Wilson, George Brown and the other Labour leaders said
when selling the incomes policy to the trade unions.

Mark II must be different to Mark I

Incomes policy Mark I completely failed to reach its three
main targets.

The National Plan, announced with such a great fanfare,
went first. 'Conceived October 1964, born September
1965, died (possibly murdered) July 1966' (R. Opie,
'Economic Planning and Growth' in W. Beckerman (ed.)
The Labour Government's Economic Record, 1964-1970,
London, 1972, p. 170).

It went in the fierce deflation that was imposed together
with a wage freeze in a frantic effort to overcome a balance
of payments crisis in July 1966. The effort failed, but the

Plan had gone, unsung and unlamented. Growth was abandoned, and instead of a 'planned growth of wages' we had a complete freeze.

The government imposed a standstill on all wage increases for six months, and then severe restraint, accompanied by harsh deflationary policies for another six months. During this stage wages were allowed to rise only under exceptional circumstances. The freeze was still on.

In the third stage, between July 1967 and March 1968, the nil norm for wage increases was replaced by a 3-3½ per cent norm, and the government took powers to delay proposed pay increases for up to six months.

A fourth stage began in April 1968. The government relinquished its power to postpone wage rises. A ceiling of 3½ per cent was imposed on all wage rises, unless specifically exempted. This stage continued, under the Prices and Incomes Act 1968, until the end of 1969. While it was on, the government retained the power to hold back wage rises beyond the 3½ per cent ceiling for up to 11 months.

Incomes policy Mark I was left high and dry, without planning or economic growth to support it.

What about the lower paid? They got nothing out of the first Wilson government. The Prices and Incomes Board was particularly mean to them. When, to take one example, the Retail Drapery Wages Council were proposing to increase the minimum wage paid to male assistants in drapers' shops from £11.15 to £11.90, the Prices and Incomes Board decided that this increase was too generous, and that £11.75 was enough (National Prices and Incomes Board, *Pay of Workers in Retail Drapery, Outfitting and Footwear,* Cmnd. 3224, 1967).

Some time later the Prices and Incomes Board showed more heart. It invoked the low-pay exception when evaluating a claim from agricultural workers who at that time were getting £10.50 for a 44-hour week. It granted a princely 3 per cent – 30p extra a week! (National Prices and Incomes Board, *Pay of Workers in Agriculture in England and Wales,* Cmnd. 3199, 1967.)

The lower paid took their revenge. They smashed to smithereens Wilson's Mark I incomes policy in autumn 1969. And then, for good measure, they repeated the performance for the February 1974 Labour government. They were having no restraint.

No government now in power can introduce a new incomes policy based on the old premises that there will be economic growth to back it up, or that it is synonymous with a planned growth of wages, or that it is aimed to help the lower paid.

New tunes are now necessary.

Nor can Wilson's Mark II use a year-long wages standstill or even a 3½ per cent guideline. These might have been alright when the rate of inflation was about 4 per cent per year; but now, when it is 17 per cent, they are simply not on. The dam will break much quicker than last time.

And finally, the government of today cannot hope to deflect the demand for straight wage rises by encouraging the introduction or spread of productivity deals. Last time productivity deals were the one legitimate loophole in the earnings norms. They were new and their use was encouraged by both the 1965 and the 1967 White Papers on prices and incomes.

Union officials, both left and right, fell over themselves to sign productivity deals. They were clearly the soft option in wage negotiations, attractive to the right as a way of selling conditions for pay without affecting its commitment to an incomes policy; and equally attractive to the left top brass as a way of opposing the incomes policy without defending workers' conditions.

But now eight million workers are already covered by productivity deals. The manning scales that were up for sale have by and large been sold. The same applies to tea breaks, shift work and payments systems. At the same time, many employers believe they made a mistake last time round. Although there was a large increase in productivity in industry as a whole, in many firms workers took the cash but did not deliver the goods in terms of increased output.

There were also unpleasant side effects for the capitalist class as a whole. Higher take-home pay for certain groups of workers fed the expectations of other groups who could not easily make productivity concessions. To this extent the deals provided part of the impetus to the 'revolt of the lower paid' in 1969 and 1970. Dustmen, teachers, car-workers already on Measured Day Work, everyone who had been left behind in the productivity rush, took to militant action to catch up.

Incomes policy Mark II will be different from Mark I. It will be accompanied by a massive propaganda effort around the theme that incomes policy is necessary to avoid cata-strophe — not to achieve a planned growth of wages, but to prevent massive unemployment and spiralling inflation. It will try to convince workers that they should not press for an improvement in living standards, but aim at best to defend existing ones.

The T U C's 'social contract' fits the bill perfectly:

Because of the restricted scope for real increase in consumption during the coming year, a principal consideration for unions would be to ensure that real incomes were maintained and that wages were protected against rises in the cost of living.

(T U C, *Collective Bargaining and the Social Contract,* 26 June 1974, p.6)

The rest follows naturally:

. . . the General Council's recommendations to negotiators in the coming period are as follows:

(i) although the groundwork is being laid for increasing con-sumption and living standards in the future, the scope for real increases in consumption at present is limited, and a central negotiating objective in the coming period will therefore be to ensure that real incomes are maintained;

(ii) this will entail claiming compensation for the rise in the cost of living since the last settlement, taking into account that threshold agreements will already have given some compensation for current price increases;

(iii) an alternative approach would be to negotiate arrangements to keep up with the cost of living during the period of the new agreement;

(iv) the 12 month interval between major increases should in general continue to apply;

(v) priority should be given to negotiating agreements which will have beneficial effects on unit costs and efficiency, to reforming pay structures, and to improving job security;

(vi) priority should also be given to attaining reasonable minimum standards, including the T U C's low-pay target of a £25 minimum basic rate with higher minimum earnings, for a normal week for those aged 18 and over;

(vii) a continuing aim is the elimination of discrimination against particular groups, notably women; improving non-wage benefits such as sick pay and occupational pension schemes, and progress towards four weeks' annual holiday;

(viii) full use should be made of the conciliation, arbitration and mediation services of the C A S to help towards a quick solution of disputes.

Thresholds — the indexed wage freeze

Up to 1966 a large number of workers were covered by cost-of-living agreements. Altogether more than two million: building workers, printers, workers in footwear manufacture, the hosiery industry, and others.

The 1964 Labour government disapproved of such arrangements. It believed they were inflationary, and having obtained the agreement of the C B I and the T U C, published its views in a White Paper, April 1965. After this, the Prices and Incomes Board frowned on all index-tied cost-of-living arrangements that came to its attention, as in the printing industry, and a court of inquiry in the hosiery industry even managed to disapprove of a scheme that had been in operation since 1919 (Court of Inquiry, no 3134, dated 13 March 1967, D E P).

The number of workers covered by cost-of-living clauses

declined very rapidly. The building industry abolished its cost-of-living arrangements (which had been in force for 40 years) in March 1967. The furniture industry replaced its cost-of-living allowance in January 1968. General Printing and Newspapers ceased to apply automatic increases to bonuses (related to price increases) between October 1967 and January 1969. Smaller groups of workers did the same. By 1969 there were only about 375,000 workers still covered by cost-of-living provisions (*Hansard*, 24 February 1969, vol. 778, no 64, col. 192), and in 1970 the number of manual workers covered had fallen to 150,000 (*Hansard*, vol. 804, no 18, Written Answer, col. 153). The Iron and Steel Industry dropped its cost-of-living arrangements finally by consolidating them with minimum rates in March 1970.

But by the end of 1970, prices were beginning to put pressure on the accepted policy. Vic Feather and the General Council of the T U C turned towards the idea of threshold agreements. In January 1971 the T U C presented a paper advocating thresholds to the National Economic Development Council: to protect the real value of wage increases, it stated, unions might want to negotiate 'agreements which provide for the upward adjustment of wage rates in the event of prices rising above a certain threshold'. It argued that, by pursuing a policy of threshold clauses and improvements in non-wage conditions, 'in place of basing immediate increases on the assumption that the pace of inflation will continue', the unions might 'help to take some force out of the immediate wage-price spiral'.

The government and the C B I did not accept the idea of a threshold clause and rejected the T U C's other ideas for dealing with inflation.

On 4 February the T U C held a conference on cost-of-living threshold agreements in London. Vic Feather, the General Secretary, argued that one of the advantages of a threshold agreement was that, while protecting workers' living standards, it would facilitate long-term agreements with management:

> Cost of living threshold clauses lend themselves particularly well to company corporate planning ... of longer-term agreements ... our present proposal is in fact even *more suitable* for long-term planning than the old style of cost-of-living clause. Some type of cost-of-living guarantee is absolutely vital for any long-term agreement. If I were the head of a large business corporation, I would be very interested in the idea of getting a degree of forward planning so far as wages and labour costs were concerned.
>
> (T U C Press Release, 4 February 1971)

By and large the union leaders received Vic Feather's suggestions without enthusiasm, even with some antagonism. The C B I was also not ready to commit itself to threshold agreements. It wanted to probe its terms and to haggle. When it finally did reach a tentative view it was lukewarm.

And there the matter lay until Heath revived the idea as a sweetener to gain trade union acceptance of Phase Three of his incomes policy. Although he miscalculated, and reached the threshold level much earlier than intended, thresholds had come to stay.

Heath's collapse and the breach of Phase Three under pressure from the miners has brought thresholds into the centre of the discussion on a new incomes policy. The prestigious National Institute of Economic and Social Research suggested that there should

> be no further general increases in wages but that a system of universal indexation would be introduced on a percentage basis (instead of the present 40p threshold for each 1 per cent rise in the Retail Price Index) whereby for each 1 per cent rise in the consumer price index there is a corresponding 1 per cent rise in gross monetary earnings from employment. This system would be operated quarterly and come into effect in the first quarter of 1975 when everyone would receive compensation for the rise in prices since the previous quarter. After the adjustment in the

first quarter money earnings remain unchanged until the second quarter, when there is again a rise in earnings to offset the rise in prices which has meanwhile occurred.

(*National Institute Economic Review*, May 1974, p. 5)
Review, May 1974, p. 5)

The conservative weekly the *Economist* came out in support. And then the idea reappeared in the T U C General Council statement of 26 June 1974 on the 'social contract'.

Threshold agreements are very dangerous for workers

For a 1 per cent rise in the cost of living 40p does not fully compensate a worker whose earnings are £40 a week. For one thing, the Retail Price Index does not properly reflect a working-class pattern of expenditure. It is based on the expenditure of an 'average household'. Most workers are below the average and different to it. At present this 'average household' is said to be spending 24.8 per cent of its income on food, 12.6 per cent on housing, 4.9 per cent on tobacco, 5.8 per cent on fuel and light, and so on. The major categories are broken down even further: housing, for example, is divided into 7.5 per cent for rent, 3.2 per cent for rates and water charges, 0.8 per cent for repairs and maintenance and 1.1 per cent for materials, decorations and so on.

According to these figures a tenant paying £5 a week rent, which is not abnormal, should be receiving a disposable income of £60 a week, which is abnormal, since it implies a gross wage of around £80 per week. The rental equivalent rule also means that rises in house prices and mortgage rates do not affect the Retail Price Index either, even though they directly affect disposable incomes for large numbers of workers.

Then again, low-income groups spend a much greater proportion of their income on food and other items whose prices have risen much faster than the general index in recent months. Between January 1972 and January 1973 when the Retail Price Index went up 7.7 per cent, housing costs rose 14 per cent, food 10.1 per cent, meals bought out (including works canteens) 10 per cent, and seasonal foods 18 per cent. All these are things on which working-class families spend a greater proportion of their income than the 'average'.

But even if the statistics were perfect, 40p would not compensate for a rise in prices of 1 per cent for a worker earning £40. Something like a third of any rise is automatically taken off in income tax and social insurance contributions. To compensate for a 1 per cent price rise, a worker really needs a 1½ per cent wage rise. And that is a low estimate. F. Wilkinson and H. A. Turner have shown that, although wage earners' gross real earnings (ie. after allowing for the increased cost of living) rose by over a third between 1959 and 1970, about half the gain was taken back in tax and social insurance deductions (see graph).

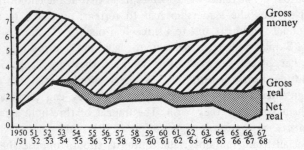

Trends in rates of increase of average gross money, gross real, and net real income, 1948-1970

Manual worker, wife and two children (D.E.P. Enquiry)

Per cent annual increase in income

Then again, even if 40p were enough to compensate for a 1 per cent wage rise in 1974, that would not be enough in 1975 or 1976. Inflation and wage rises together will have reduced its relative importance in the wage packet.

The threshold system of payment cheats the worker in yet another way — it does not compensate for the rise in prices that takes place up to the time the threshold payment is triggered. In this way, threshold agreements are worse than the old cost-of-living sliding scale agreements. Finally, threshold payments do not take account of over-time or shift-working: 40p is paid and that's it, regardless of how many hours and what kind of shift you work.

The threshold system of payment could have a very serious long-run effect on shop floor organization. It could encourage British employers to emulate some of the methods used in the United States, for instance, to impose long-term agreements and castrate the stewards' organization.

It was under the cover of a sliding scale cost-of-living clause in 1948 that the leaders of the United Auto Workers dared to push through a two-year agreement with General Motors, instead of the annual agreement that was custom-ary. Then in 1950, in the midst of the roaring inflation induced by the Korean war, they went even further and signed a new five-year agreement, once again shielding themselves behind a sliding scale cost-of-living clause. The uproar in the ranks was so widespread that at the end of the five years the leadership had to retreat; not, alas, to an annual agreement, but to a three-year one.

Similar long-term agreements have been introduced in other places of work. For workers they are dangerous during runaway inflation. **Workers should insist on all agreements being open-ended, so that they can terminate them whenever they wish.** The impact of threshold agree-ments on workers' organization is the main reason why socialist and militant trade unionists should oppose them utterly. **We must oppose any and every attempt to replace wage battles with statistical argument between trade union and government bureaucrats. In the final analysis no mech-anism of wage determination can replace trade union**

strength deployed to achieve real wage rises.

Threshold clauses are a threat to more than factory organization. They tend to suppress profits as a factor in wage negotiations. They tend to orientate workers towards the defence of existing standards rather than towards improving them and cutting into the level of profits. **Socialists and active trade unionists should completely oppose the threshold system of payments for what it is — an indexed wage freeze.** *

Lower-paid workers

Priority should also be given to attaining reasonable minimum standards, including the TUC's low-pay target of a £25 minimum basic rate with higher minimum earnings, for a normal week for those aged 18 and over; a continuing aim is the elimination of discrimination against particular groups, notably women.

(The TUC statement on the 'social contract')

Many workers believe that incomes policy is a good thing in principle, even if they don't agree that it applies to themselves at present. Many believe that it makes sense for better off workers to practise restraint in order to improve lower-paid workers' wages. But in fact the whole idea is based on a misunderstanding: if I C I workers were to hold back on a claim for another £1 a week, would the management of I C I transfer the money they had saved to, say, the nurses, or would they transfer it into I C I's bank

---

* The above argument seems at first sight to contradict the position that *Socialist Worker* took encouraging demands for the threshold payments available under Phase Three. There would have been a contradiction if *Socialist Worker* had encouraged workers to believe that threshold payments were enough. But it did not. Instead it recognized that many workers did not yet feel strongly enough to take on both the employer and the law. But workers did feel able to take on the employer alone over the one sort of extra payment allowed under Phase Three. Success in such struggles could only help them build up the muscle, the organization and the confidence to fight seriously once Phase Three ended.

account? We have only to ask the question to see what the answer is. In fact, the way wages are won under capitalism is quite simple: workers in the strongest sections, in the technologically advanced industries, where they are best organized, win increases; and the rest of the working class keep up by the simple process of comparing their own wages with those received by the strongest and best paid.

If a worker in a strong position gets a small wage rise, the one in a weaker position will get even less. This is why wage differences within the working class have declined considerably over the years as the workers' strength grew: skilled workers that were getting twice as much as the unskilled for years prior to 1914 were only 15 or 10 per cent ahead by the fifties in Britain (K. G. J. C. Knowles, 'Wages and Productivity' in G. D. N. Worswick and P. H. Ady (eds., *The British Economy in the 1950s*, London, 1962). It also explains why wage differences are so huge in the backward countries where workers' organization is poor and trade union rights not secure.

If anything was needed to explode the myth that incomes policy would act as the angel of social justice for the lower-paid workers, it was the Prices and Incomes Board's refusal of the railwaymen in January 1966. In their report, wages per standard week (excluding overtime) were given as follows: porters, £10.18s; leading luggage room attendant, £12.5s; second-year guard, £12.19s; qualified firemen £14.8s; qualified train driver, £16.19s (National Board for Prices and Incomes, *Pay and Conditions of Service of British Railways Staff*, Cmnd. 2873, January 1966, pp. 32-33). There they are, low-paid grades in plenty – but still no suggestion that more pay should be given to the wretchedly underpaid sections.

The different sections of the working class are standing on different wage escalators; the speed at which one escalator moves affects the speeds of all the others, and in the same direction. If one accelerates, so do the others; if

Socialist Worker, 13 October 1973

one is held back, so will the others be.

The strongest and best-organized workers must not hold back, for if they do the whole working class will be held back with them.

Fight for a minimum wage

The trade union movement must go beyond the concept of the wage escalator. The stronger sections should give direct help to the weaker ones.

In this respect the T U C has behaved absolutely abominably. Again and again the T U C has passed resolutions on the attainment of a minimum basic wage. In 1971 it declared its support for a minimum of £20 per week. In 1973 the figure was raised to £25. Recently, in September 1974, it was raised again, to £30.

All well and good. But what are the *actual* wages of workers? How many of them are below the minimum target of the T U C?

In 1973 over one third of all male manual workers and 86.3 per cent of all female manual workers earned a basic wage of less than £25 per week (Fisher and Dix, pp. 69-71, 94-95). 56 per cent of non-manual women workers and some 15 per cent of non-manual male workers also earned less than the minimum target.

The T U C has done nothing to press for a statutory minimum wage. Whenever the unions of the lower paid raise the issue at trade union and Labour Party conferences, they are rebuffed by the leaders of other unions.

At the 1973 Labour Party Conference, Alan Fisher, General Secretary of the National Union of Public Employees, moved a resolution calling on the party to commit itself to establishing a minimum wage once it was returned to power.

The resolution was opposed from the floor of the conference by John Boyd, the right-wing leader of the Amalgamated Union of Engineering Workers, and from the platform — for the National Executive — by Tom Bradley, an M P sponsored by the Transport Salaried Staffs Association. The big battalions dutifully fell into line and defeated Fisher's resolution.

The rejection of this and other similar resolutions was repeated again at trade union conferences that year, notwithstanding the fact that there is a long-standing clause in the T U C's constitution, included in every annual report, specifically stating that one of the organization's objectives shall be to endeavour to establish 'a legal minimum wage for each industry or occupation'. John Boyd's excuse used at the 1973 Labour Party Conference, that the trade unions oppose on principle government interference with collective bargaining, won't wash — one can oppose anti-working-class laws, and still demand the eight-hour day.

The T U C does not press for a statutory minimum wage is because to do so would be to put a Labour government on the spot. And it is for this reason that the 'social contract' does not call for a statutory minimum wage, and contains only a vague statement of intent.

The T U C recommends that negotiations should aim at Wages not rising, except for the lower paid in the coming period;

Cost-of-living agreements to compensate for rising prices;

12-month intervals between agreements.

As against this militant trade unionists and socialists should fight for:

- **£35 per week minimum wage;**
- **30 per cent across-the-board wage rises;**
- **No time limit to any agreement; the right to renegotiate whenever the workers demand it.**

The 'social contract' is doomed

Harold Wilson tried a voluntary incomes policy when he first came to office. It fell to pieces in the rebellion of the lower paid in 1969. This time, with inflation four or five times higher than last, his incomes policy will be doomed even faster.

Talk of its fairness cannot stick when workers read about nine-carat gold neckchains — for cats — price £85 (*Observer* magazine, 20 May 1974); or velvet 'Marie Antoinette' kennels for £140, and small doggy winter coats — in mink — from £400 at Harrods (London, *Evening News,* 10 December 1973); or penthouse suites at £35,900 each, on the QE2's 1975 91-day round-the-world cruise (*Daily Mail*, 25 January 1974); or Michael Noble, Tory M P for Argyllshire's bottle of Chateau Mouton Rothschild, which went for a record £3,538 (£100 a glass) (*Daily Express*, 24 May 1972).

What happens to fairness when such facts are compared with ones like:

● On Christmas Day, 1972, an old age pensioner, Mrs Mary McCloy, was found dead in her flat, choked to death on cardboard. There was no food in the house.

● Long queues of pensioners form each morning outside Greggs' bakery shop in Westgate Road, Newcastle. The reason? Stale bread and cakes returned from the firm's other shops are sold to the pensioners for half price. A spokesman for the firm said that previously 'the bread used to be destroyed and it was normal for it to be sent to pig farms' (*Morning Star*, 17 July 1974).

Pegged wages will look grim on a background of massive profits for individual companies. Even if only a few companies announce increases, as B P, Shell, I C I and the banks have done this year, it will be enough to fuel the resentment of workers bound by the 'social contract'.

This time round, workers will know more about what is going on. The heavier the government propaganda, the more press and television discuss the 'social contract,' the more workers find out about who broke it and how. There is hardly a worker who did not hear about the Ford wage claim during and after the election in October. Now that wages have become the football of commentators and politicians wage battles have become public property. They are carried out in a goldfish bowl. Workers see more and know more and are more willing to push for comparability and parity.

If the 'social contract' is accompanied by rising unemployment, then the unfairness of the situation will be even more blatant, and the rebellion against the 'social contract' will break out even more quickly and sharply.

Workers are also more suspicious. The fact that, on the eve of the October general election, there was a fantastic strike wave, shows how little leeway they will allow for government, including a Labour government.

With inflation running at a rate of 15-20 per cent, any sugar on the pill of the 'social contract' will lose its taste for most workers in a very short time. If the 'social contract' is accompanied by rising unemployment, it will take even less time. In 1969 it was the workers with no traditional militancy or strength of organization that broke through the wage restraint. This time the breakthrough will come much more quickly, and through the activity of workers on a much wider front, from relatively well-paid car workers to ancillary workers in hospitals.

4.
The Threat of Unemployment

The economics experts all expect unemployment to rise this winter, and again next winter.

Unemployment in Britain is already higher than in most industrial countries. It does not appear to be because it is measured in a peculiar way, by registration at the Labour Exchange rather than directly. But if it is measured in the same way as in other countries, unemployment in Britain is one of the highest in the world. At the end of 1971, and using the U S method of calculation, it compared as follows:

Britain	5.3 per cent
Italy	3.4 per cent
France	2.7 per cent
West Germany	0.7 per cent
Japan	1.3 per cent
United States	5.9 per cent

From: National Institute of Economic and Social Research, *Economic Review,* February 1973, p.69.

Unemployment has jumped up in two fairly steep movements in the last ten years; the first in 1967, the second in 1971. The number of wholly unemployed males in Britain, seasonally adjusted, rose from a little over 200,000 in early 1966 to over 700,000 in 1971.

We are now at the beginning of the third big push since the Second World War in the level of unemployment.

Softening the resistance to sacking

In 1965 the Labour government introduced the Redundancy Payments Act. It was meant to encourage workers to accept sackings without fuss. And it worked. A study of the Act five years later showed that it really did undermine militancy and the capacity of shop stewards to lead opposition to redundancy; and that the number of strikes about redundancy had declined although the number of instances of redundancy rose sharply: while the number of working days lost through all strikes went up by a quarter between 1960-65 and 1966-69, the average number of working days lost each year through redundancy strikes dropped from 161,774 to only 74,473. As the study noted, 'the Act had made it easier for many employers to discharge workers, largely because it enabled them to dismiss men with an easier conscience, and reduce costs and argument' (S. R. Parker, C. G. Thomas, N. D. Ellis and W. E. J. McCarthy, *Effects of the Redundancy Payments Act,* London, 1971).

Socialist Worker, 21 April 1973

But things are changing. Redundancy is no longer so easy for the employers. Since the work-in at U C S, the idea of occupying a factory as an answer to it has become more and more popular. But before dealing with that, let us look at another 'solution' to unemployment – the one suggested and encouraged by Anthony Wedgwood Benn.

Workers' co-operatives

The idea has been tried on three separate occasions – at the Norton Villiers Triumph motorcycle factory at Meriden, near Coventry; at the *Scottish Daily Express* Glasgow; and at the former Fisher-Bendix factory near Liverpool, now owned by I P D.

Anthony Wedgwood Benn was exuberant about the Meriden experiment. It was, he said, 'a new chapter in the history of industrial organization and relations in this country'. The government offered the Meriden co-operative £4,950,000 subject to 'concluding the necessary agreements, including terms of business with the owners, Norton Villiers, Triumph'. A similar offer of £1¾ million was made to the former workers on the *Scottish Daily Express* to launch the *Scottish Daily News*, conditional on their raising a similar sum to buy out Beaverbrook interests.

Quite naturally the workers facing redundancy at these places see in the government suggestions a way out of their difficulties. But there is a grave danger involved in these experiments.

The Meriden project pinpoints some of them. The co-operative is to buy £4 million of the £7 million worth of N V T assets at Meriden. This will swallow up most of the government loan. The other £3 million of assets will be removed by N V T. The co-operative will then work, in effect, as a sub-contractor to N V T which will also market its output. To fulfil the production plans will require a staggering increase in the intensity of work. As the *Sunday Times* reported, in an article entitled 'Meriden – Tough

Targets',

> So far undisclosed plans are to turn out 12,000 bikes with a
> workforce of 450 in the first year, stepping up employment to
> 750 to double output in 1975. As Meriden has never turned out
> more than 30,000 machines with 1,750 men on the payroll
> under previous managements, this is a productivity boost of at
> least 85 per cent.
> (28 July 1974)

In short, the workers are to drive themselves harder,
much harder, than they ever did under the previous management. They are to accept flexibility, mobility, inter-
changeability. And the profit from their labour will go to
the state (in interest charges and repayments) and to N V T
which sells the bikes.

It was inevitable. As an editorial in *Socialist Worker* put
it:

> You cannot build islands of socialism in a sea of capitalism, and
> workers' management of a commercial concern operated in that
> sea deprives the workers of the strength of union organization
> directed against management.
> (20 July 1974)

As for the second case – the *Scottish Daily Express* –
the printing unions are worried that its operations will
undermine resistance to cutting the labour force in other
newspapers:

> ... the old *Express* operation employed nearly 2,000 people in
> Glasgow. The new paper would only have 500. If it succeeded, it
> could make the manning levels of other British national news-
> papers look bloated indeed.
> (*Sunday Times*, 25 August 1974)

Using unemployment to discipline workers

While the Labour leaders are still trying to soften the
effects of unemployment through using the Redundancy
Payments Act (1965), bailing out bankrupt companies like
Ferranti, and encouraging workers' co-operatives, some of
the Tory leaders have started toying with the idea of *using*

unemployment to damp down inflation by cutting workers' wage demands and militancy.

The main spokesman of this group is Sir Keith Joseph, and their main line, in his words:

> We cannot talk about fighting inflation as the overriding priority and then in the same or another speech say that we cannot take monetary action which might threaten more jobs. We cannot have it both ways.

> If the money supply is held down then after three or four years the country's economy will be on a sounder basis.
>
> *(The Times,* 6 September 1974)

That Sir Keith Joseph's theory is nonsense doesn't make it less dangerous.

It is nonsense because it doesn't fit the facts.

● As unemployment in Britain rose, the rate of inflation went up, not down:

	Real unemployment rate* per cent	Rate of inflation per cent per year
1961-65	2.6	3.6
1966-70	3.5	4.6
1971	5.6	9.9

*Using the US method of measuring unemployment.

(Unemployment figures from National Institute of Economic and Social Research, *Economic Review,* May 1971, p.67; inflation figures from OECD, *Main Economic Indicators,* 1971.)

● As unemployment rose, the level of strike activity went up, now down. As the *Economist* put it:

> a record number of days were lost in 1972, which was a year that began with one million unemployed. In America fewer days were lost during the last boom than during the last recession. There could even be a tendency now for unemployment to be associated with more severe strikes.
>
> (21 September 1974)

Unemployment is less of a whip than it used to be. The strength of workers' organization means that it no longer automatically reduces the willingness of workers to push for wage improvements. Tightly organized groups of workers, strategically placed at the centre of the system, are not going to be intimidated by lengthening dole queues at the periphery. At the same time the measures government introduces to make unemployment more acceptable — redundancy payments, wage-related dole, and so on — serve only to diminish its disciplinary effect.

Factory occupations

A turning point in the struggle against sackings came with the occupation of U C S in July 1971. U C S captured the imagination of millions. The response was incredible. Money poured in and so did messages of support. On 18 August 80,000 people marched through Glasgow, and an estimated 200,000 went on a token strike — in solidarity with the U C S workers.

Since then there have been many other factory occupations to stop sackings and factory closures. Plesseys in Alexandria; Fisher-Bendix; Don Steel Works; Pressed Steel Fisher in Washwood Heath, Birmingham; Briant Colour Printing in London; B S A in Birmingham; Norton Villiers Triumph in Meriden; *Scottish Daily Express* in Glasgow; Strachan Engineering in Eastleigh; McLaren Controls in Glasgow; Baynard's Press (subsidiary of the giant I P C) in London; Thorneycroft (subsidiary of Leyland) in Basingstoke; Stanmore Engineering in Wembley; Allis Chalmers in North Wales; Seiko Time in London; Harris Engineering in Tunbridge Wells; and others.

Although rare in Britain until three years ago, sit-in strikes are not new. A huge wave of sit-ins swept through the United States in the last half of the thirties. The most famous of them all began in the General Motors factories in Flint in December 1936. It went on for 44 days, and ended with a complete victory for the workers. It was a central event in the rise of the Congress of Industrial Organizations,

and in the spread of trade unionism in the United States.
The sit-in strike can be incredibly effective:

> U S workers found the sit-down to have many advantages over
> the traditional forms of strike. It prevents the use of scabs to
> operate a factory, since the strikers guard the machines. It is
> harder for the company to oust men from inside a plant than
> break through an encircling picket line. Bosses are more reluct-
> ant to resort to strike-breaking violence, because it directly
> endangers millions of dollars of company property, vast as-
> sembly lines and unfinished products.
>
> In a sit-down the workers' morale is heightened. They are inside
> and therefore know for certain that scabs are not operating the
> machines; they are really protecting their jobs and this leads to a
> higher degree of solidarity and militancy. The men are protected
> from the weather. They are never scattered, but are always on
> call at a moment's notice in case of trouble. The basic demo-
> cratic character of the sit-down is guaranteed by the fact that the
> workers on the line, rather than outside officials, determine its
> course.
>
> (W. Linder, *The Great Flint Sit-Down Strike against GM
> 1936-1937,* Solidarity pamphlet, 1969, pp. 3-4)

But the potentialities of the sit-in are not always used. In
many factory occupations in Britain, from U C S onwards,
the leadership did not understand that sit-in tactics demand
mass, active involvement of the rank and file:

> Because a sit-in does not need the traditional forms of picketing
> and does not rely on the same kind of regular mass meetings to
> organize itself that a strike does, it can easily slump into
> demanding less activity, commitment and democracy than a
> normal dispute.
>
> When this attitude is compounded with a carefully controlled
> absence of apparent employer and police hostility, an absence of
> any campaign for solidarity and a predominantly defensive
> character defining the whole struggle, then the actual level of
> militancy can be lower than a normal strike.
>
> (Roger Rosewell, 'Sit-ins – the Experience', *International Social-
> ism,* no 53, October-December 1972)

In a number of factory occupations no active militant

involvement of the workers took place. Thus, at U C S, according to Rosewell,

> The role allotted to the rank and file was overwhelmingly passive. Thus whilst the leaders spoke, travelled and argued, the workers were only required to work, wait and attend occasional mass meetings that were themselves more a part of the publicity campaign than a democratic assembly which would decide between alternative tactics. The policy of the government was also important, for it decided that at no stage in the crisis would it precipitate a showdown, and in this it was considerably aided by the shop stewards' committee's refusal to increase the tempo of the struggle. The management was still allowed disciplinary powers; no ships were seized and then held until firm guarantees about the future of the yards were forthcoming and not one single meeting of West of Scotland stewards was convened in the yards in defiance of capitalist trespass laws. In truth, neither party wanted a showdown and the efforts of each to avoid one both complemented and reinforced the circumstances by which it was prevented.

Defensive tactics in the face of factory closures are simply no good. The article concludes:

> Clearly if an employer intends to close an establishment he has little need for it to be used as a productive unit and therefore its value, apart from the plant and machinery, is less than before. Under such circumstances, and with a policy decision not to attempt forcible eviction, there is a grave danger that an employer's strategy of adopting a superficial patience and then relying upon the apparent lack of progress, and such factors as boredom, routine, and financial hardship to sufficiently weaken the workers' resolve, will either allow a sudden eviction or a negotiated settlement that only applies to a minority or largely reduced percentage of the original workforce.

How to organize a factory occupation effectively

The most useful advice on the subject was given by the rank and file paper, the *Carworker:*

If the employer gives you reasonable advance notice of redundancy or factory closure, preparation can be of vital importance. The stewards' committee should elect a sub-committee from among its members whose responsibility it is to draw up plans for a possible sit-in.

Meanwhile, steps should be taken to stop work being moved out of the factory. If the factory votes to take unspecified action in the future, then the organization of a levy to build up a fund would be extremely valuable.

If very little notice is given, the reaction depends to a great extent on the traditions of the factory organization, and on the quality of the leadership.

But once a vote is taken in favour of occupation there should be no hanging around allowing outside parties to sow doubts. Occupation should start immediately.

The action taken in the first hour will be quite crucial in determining the limits of the struggle. The management and supervision must be evicted immediately.

The factory offices must be taken over. Barricades must be erected at the gates, and an immediate security system instituted to control movement in and out of the factory.

The factory meeting should then be reconvened and the necessary tasks spelt out. An occupation committee should be elected. A rota for sitting-in must be worked out.

And if the offices are held, and therefore the insurance cards controlled, a democratic decision should be taken on whether the insurance cards should be frozen, thus ensuring that the struggle is not undermined by people drifting away.

For the first week daily mass meetings should be held to make sure that the whole thing is being organized properly.

Committees should be appointed to deal with crucial organizational matters such as security, money, information, food, cleaning, health, entertainment, etc. The whole workforce must be involved in one or other of the tasks.

The rota system for sitting-in should make sure that there is always a fixed minimum number inside the factory, and that all the main needs are catered for.

Apart from active involvement, money is another crucial aspect of the operation. Financial hardship may become a serious weakening factor.

If the occupation has been made official, then one or two members from each union represented must immediately fill in the necessary applications and make every effort to see they are acted upon. Where dispute benefit is a long time in coming, then what money is available should be pooled.

As strike pay is not sufficient, collection sheets must be produced from the start, and sent out over as wide an area as possible. Fund-raising delegations should also be sent out to collect from local factories and from factories in the industry nationally.

Speakers should be sent to all local trade union branch meetings to request financial assistance. Obviously, where possible, the organization of a weekly levy in sympathetic factories would be a great advantage.

The financial resources of the unions must be brought to bear in the dispute. In the T & G W U the executive has the power to organize levies.

In the A U E W, the local district committee can take a district ballot vote over whether a weekly levy of up to 5p per member should be raised for an approved dispute. They can also, with the E C's consent, appeal to other districts not directly involved to hold ballots for a levy.

The money collected from other factories should be established as a fund on which those members in the greatest hardship have the first right to draw. Those with next right should be those prepared to do the more unpleasant tasks.

It should be a democratically decided rule that those who do not participate in the sit-in in any way should not receive any financial benefit apart from strike pay.

Where possible, every attempt should be made to get the members along to the factory. A U E W vacant books should be kept on the premises for example.

As well as money from these sources, everyone should be able to find out about social security benefits and tax rebates. Committees should be formed to deal with these questions.

One way of explaining your case locally will be through the organization of demonstrations, where the placards are well designed and to the point. Leaflets explaining your case should be handed out at every opportunity.

And the involvement of wives and families should be considered an important priority, because neglect of members' domestic problems can help undermine the will to fight.

Regular wives' meetings should be held, where they are kept in the picture. Socials can also be organized on the premises, and also outside the factory. Fund-raising can be supplemented by raffles, etc.

Every use should be made of the company offices. Apart from using the telephone, assuming sympathetic post office engineers refuse to cut you off, a substantial amount of dirt can probably be gathered on the company. This should be made as widely known as possible.

To guard against a possible eviction, the machines can be immobilized and key tools hidden or smuggled out.

The main point is to involve the members in regular activity. Apart from general duties inside the factory, cultural activity should flourish. This means putting on plays, showing films, organizing lectures and so on.

It is very important at the beginning to invite down trade unionists who have been involved in sit-ins themselves.

Aside from the whole organization necessary to sustain the struggle is the adoption of tactics outside the factory that can help to win the struggle.

This is very important, because in cases where the whole plant is to be closed down, apart from the value of the machinery the employers can sit back and hope you bore yourselves to death because he knows that property values are going up all the time. So by delaying his sale you are only doing him a good turn.

Through official and unofficial channels solidarity action has to be arranged. If there is an alternative source of supply for your product, get it blacked both at source and where it's worked on.

If this proves unsuccessful then the tactic of flying picket can be used — first of all leafleting the workers involved, talking to them as they go into work and so on. If this fails, start stopping supplies going into the factory. Someone will react to that.

If there are any spare depots then seek to neutralize them by organizing blacking plus a certain amount of picketing.

If you are part of a combine, it is necessary to try to grind it to a halt — with the men's co-operation. If all else fails try to get a more important factory occupied.

And the final card, which can be played at any time, the earlier the better, is to occupy the administrative and financial centre of the company — getting fellow trade unionists to mount a mass picket to prevent your eviction.

('How a Sit-in is Organized', *Carworker,* October-November 1972)

Revolutionary potential of factory occupations

Factory occupations challenge the right of the bosses to run the factories. They challenge their right to own productive property. They go so far as to challenge the capitalist system itself. **Factory occupations are a political weapon, and must be led politically. They must be turned not only against the employer but against the government of the day, and against the capitalist system itself.** If the bosses cannot run the economy without sackings, the workers can.

The main demands in the fight against unemployment:

- **Five days' work or five days' pay;**
- **35-hour week now — for 40 hours' wages;**
- **Nationalization of industry without compensation to be run under workers' control.**

5.
The Attack on the Social Services

What the capitalists cannot accomplish by their direct assault on wages, they will try to make good on another front, where the workers are more vulnerable: the social wage — pensions, education, health services, and welfare. These are as much part of the real income of working-class families as the wage packet.

We have referred to the fact that on the wages front workers who are well placed to make gains prepare the ground for those who are not quite so well placed and provide them with a target to aim at. But there are some people in the working class who have nothing at all to fight with, people who can't hope to keep up without help.

These people are the old age pensioners, the sick, the mentally deficient, unskilled workers with large families, single-parent families — all of them with little or no bargaining power. To them class solidarity could mean most in terms of their standard of living; and yet they are the ones who gain least from it at the moment. They represent, in all, 15 per cent of the population.

Social services — how much?

The period immediately after the Second World War was the high-water mark for the social services from the workers' point of view. The bosses had been frightened into it during the war. As Quintin Hogg, now Lord Hailsham, put it to the House of Commons (17 February 1943):

> If you do not give the people reform, they are going to give you social revolution. Let anyone consider the possibility of a series of dangerous industrial strikes, following the present hostilities, and the effect it would have on our industrial recovery.

(Quoted in N. Harris, 'The Decline of Welfare', *International Socialism,* no 7, winter 1961)

Ever since then, slowly but surely, the welfare services have been cut back – to make room for profits or to save on taxes. Occasionally, in order to help the trade union leaders carry their members into the concession chamber, or before elections, social security expenditure has gone up, but never enough to stop its long-term erosion.

As a welfare state Britain now compares badly with the rest of Western Europe:

Social security expenditure as a percentage of gross national product

West Germany	16.1
Sweden	13.8
Belgium	15.2
France	15.4
Italy	13.9
Netherlands	13.4
United Kingdom	11.8

From: J. C. Kincaid, *Poverty and Equality in Britain,* Penguin, 1973, pp.30-31.
The figures in the table are for the years 1958 to 1960, but it is highly probable that, despite a rise in welfare expenditure here, the gap between Britain and the Continent has grown even greater over the past decade.

The figures in the table are for the years 1958 to 1960, but it is highly probable that, despite a rise in welfare expenditure here, the gap between Britain and the Continent has grown even greater over the past decade.

Old age pensions

Because old age pensioners have no industrial power at all, and notwithstanding the hullabaloo about their needs, they are as badly off compared with the average worker as they were 40 years ago.

Old age pensions as a proportion of average wages

	Single-person pension per week	Average weekly earnings for manual work	Pension as % of earnings
1937	£0.50	£3.00	17
1948	£1.30	£7.05	18
1964	£3.37	£18.95	18
1966	£4.00	£20.65	19
1968	£4.50	£23.60	19
1970	£5.00	£28.90	17

From: Kincaid, p.13.

They live on the whole in appalling conditions:

● Diet. Recent surveys sponsored by the Royal College of General Practitioners reveal that four out of five elderly people show signs of vitamin deficiency.

● Housing. The 1971 Census showed that out of eight million pensioners in Britain, about three million live in houses built before 1919.

One in five of old age pensioners do not have an inside toilet, and one in six do not have a fixed bath in their house.

● Heating. The Department of Health and Social Security insists that, 'to keep old people warm in winter, the living-room temperature should be about 70°F when the temperature outside is 30°F. Bathrooms and bedrooms should be kept at the same temperature if possible.' The *British Medical Journal* for 27 January 1972 reports the results of a national survey of the house temperatures of old people. Three out of four old people had a living-room temperature of less than 65°F. Nearly two out of five lived at less than 60.8°F, which is the minimum temperature laid down in the Offices, Shops and Railways Act. One in ten pensioners had living rooms at less than 53.5°F. The research team reported that nearly 10 per cent of the sample of pensioners studied had both body temperatures of 96°F. This is only 1°F above the

77

hypothermia level.

This research study was intended to be only the first of a series of inquiries, but the government withdrew financial support, and the work has had to be stopped.

There is a special heating allowance on supplementary benefit: 30p a week for those who cannot move around easily or whose home is difficult to heat; 60p if both these factors apply; and there is a top rate of 90p a week for those who are permanently confined to bed or seriously ill.

There is no information on the number of pensioners who are currently receiving one of these heating allowances. The latest available figures are for November 1971, when 159,000 people got a heating allowance. That is one pensioner in every 50. At that time only 2,000 of the eight million pensioners got the top rate.

Medical experts say that hypothermia is the direct cause of 20,000 deaths a year. And a further 60,000 – 300 a day in the six winter months – die of diseases brought on by or aggravated by cold.

OLD MRS HORROCKS WASN'T GASSED - SHE HADN'T GOT A SHILLING FOR THE ELECTRIC FIRE...

Child care

The meanness of our rulers is as great at the other end of the age scale.

Working-class children were amongst the early sacrificial lambs of Harold Wilson's first administration. In 1967 school meals were put up from 1s to 1s 6d, and two years later by another 3d. In 1966 welfare milk for expectant mothers and young children went up from 2d to 6d a pint. In 1968 free milk for secondary school children was abolished. In the same year prescription charges were reintroduced (at 2s 6d for each item), and dental charges were increased (J. Kincaid, 'The Decline of the Welfare State', in N. Harris and J. Palmer (eds.), *World Crisis,* London, 1971, p. 58).

But the neglect of children has no party bias, as is clearly shown by the following table:

Government expenditure on school milk and welfare foods

	School milk	Welfare foods
1967-68	£18 million	£50 million
1970-71	£16 million	£46 million
1972-73	£9 million	£14 million

From: *Annual Abstract of Statistics,* 1973, Table 35, p.51.

There has been no increase in family allowances since 1968. These are now about half as important as they were then to the working-class family. As a percentage of the average industrial wage (for a family of three children) they have fallen as follows:

1968	7.8
1969	7.3
1970	6.4
1971	5.8
1972	5.0
1973	4.4
1974	4.1

From: Department of Employment and Productivity, *Gazette,* July 1974.

Of course, children in lower-paid families are eligible for the Family Income Supplement introduced in 1971 but, since it is means tested and requires a special application, more than half of those eligible do not get it.

Education

Working-class children get only *half the amount* of schooling upper-class children get — 11 years (5-16) as against about 22 (starting nursery about 2, ending university about 24). During this period their educational environment is grossly inferior. The recent cuts in the education services will hit them above all.

Look at the present position in one area — Newham:

> There is a serious staff shortage, although this is not admitted by the Director of Education. Sixty children have no school places at all and hundreds of pupils are being sent home every day. At Lister Comprehensive at least 120 kids are sent home daily, at Little Ilford 150, at Cumberland a similar number, and at St Bonaventure's 25 per cent receive no education.
>
> (*Rank and File*, a paper of socialists in the N U T, no 32, May-June 1974)

Look at another area. Essex County Council spends twice as much money sending a few pupils to *private* schools than it does on the children in the state sector:

> In 1972-73 Essex spent £451 a head on sending 40 children to Saffron Walden Friends School. It spent a further £582 per pupil at Brentwood Boys School. On its 217,340 state pupils it spent an average of £259 a head.
>
> While Essex maintains or subsidizes nearly 2,000 children's independent education, it has only 610 state nursery places.
>
> Out of the total public subsidy of £500,000 last year, £256,093 was spent on 'helping out' in just two of the so-called independent schools in the area. Another £50,000 out of the total went on rate concessions and tax rebates on covenants, insurance and grandfather school-fee payments.
>
> (*Rank and File*, no 28, December 1973)

And this at a time when £182 million (20 per cent of the total) was lopped off the education budget by the Tories (and not restored by Labour); when the teacher training colleges, in spite of desperate shortages, are being closed or drastically cut; when money for teaching materials is being reduced everywhere (by £48 million altogether) while there is a staggering rise of 37.5 per cent in their cost (1973-74); when there isn't even a roof above their heads for many children all over the country (in Bradford 51 per cent of schools have 'temporary' classroom huts, 7 per cent not even 'temporary' accommodation); when the majority of primary classes have more than 35 children, the six year old N U T target; when school meals are having their protein content reduced.

Previous penny-pinching government policies led to the collapse of a school roof in Camden in 1973 and in Stepney in 1974. Miraculously no-one was killed. There are known to be at least 180 other buildings — over 100 of which are used for educational purposes — which could have a similar fault.

The Department of Education and Science knows the names of the schools and the local authorities but will not reveal them. A matter of life and death? They are only state schools, after all. Why cause 'alarm and despondency unnecessarily', says the Department of Education and Science. (*Rank and File,* no 33, September 1974).

Housing

The standard of working-class housing has been very low for a long time. In recent years it has deteriorated.

Wilson's first government did little to improve it. Although its record was better than that of the Tory governments that preceded and followed, its target of 500,000 houses was never reached.

What *was* achieved was Centrepoint, built under Wilson and kept empty throughout his first term of office.

The Tories plunged us still deeper into homelessness: in 1973 only 293,600 houses were completed, the lowest level since 1947!

Labour or Tory, housebuilding in Britain lags very much behind other Western European countries:

Houses completed per 1,000 inhabitants

	Nether-lands	France	West Germany	Den-mark	Ire-land	Italy	UK
1969	9.6	8.6	8.3	10.2	4.8	5.3	6.8
1970	9.0	8.9	7.9	10.2	4.6	7.0	6.5
1971	10.4	9.3	9.1	10.0	5.2	6.7	6.5
1972	11.5	10.9	10.7	10.0	7.0	4.4	5.9

From: *EEC Report on Development of Social Situation in the Community in 1973*, Brussels, February 1974, p.228.

SOCIALIST WORKER FUEL CRISIS CHRISTMAS QUIZ
WHICH OF THE TWO ABOVE IS AN "ESSENTIAL SERVICE"?

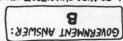

GOVERNMENT ANSWER: B

Socialist Worker, 16 December 1973

The National Health Service

The facts included in this section are from a *Socialist Worker* industrial pamphlet: *What is Happening to Our Health Service?* (November 1974).

The NHS has never been given enough money to provide the sort of medical service we need. Last December, the Tory government cut the NHS budget by £111 million, a severe blow to comprehensive free health treatment for working people. Inflation is in danger of administering the final blow.

The Lancet, voice of the medical establishment and a journal not given to overstatement, warns:

> The economic state of the NHS is far more serious than indicated by the £111 million cut... Simply to restore a devaluing NHS budget would require an *extra* £125-30 million a year.

The hospital building programme has been rendered meaningless. Every new building has a question mark against it. Every hospital board has had to submit a list of cuts, from new porters' messes to new district hospitals. At the same time, hospitals are being closed at a record rate, 38 in 1972 alone.

Yet new hospitals are desperately needed. Nearly half of Britain's hospital buildings were built before 1891, and nearly a quarter are more than 100 years old. Only four mental hospitals have been built since 1915. New coats of paint and modern direction signs can't disguise Poor Law architecture.

The hospitals that do exist are in danger of seizing up because of staff shortages. The government issues no up-to-date figures – they would be too frightening – but the Confederation of Health Service Employees estimates a shortage of 70,000 nurses, missing because the NHS can't pay them a living wage.

While the NHS is starved of funds, the private pharmaceutical industry is having a field day, bleeding the health services by charging exorbitant prices for medicines.

In 1970 Roche commanded eight-ninths of the British tranquilizer market, had an annual turnover of over £500 million, declared a profit of £84 million, and had its £1 ordinary shares valued on the Stock Market at £23,000 each. It was finally investigated by the Monopolies Commission, which found that each kilo of Valium cost £100 to make and was sold to the N H S for £1,962, and that the company had embezzled £12,877,000 of the N H S's money over and above a generous allowance for profits and research costs.

But when the Tory government tried to recover some of this money, the company, which has offices in Switzerland, Uruguay and Canada, refused point blank. It was backed up by the House of Lords and by the quality newspapers.

Although Roche's 2,000 per cent profit is a little exceptional, the average rate of profit for the drug industry is huge, the highest for any group of companies in the country. In 1970-71, Cynamid returned 43.2 per cent, Boots 28.1 per cent, and Beechams 24.5 per cent. Recently, the drug giant Glaxo was the subject of a vicious take-over battle. So rich were the potential pickings that in 12 weeks the total share value increased by £110 million.

The field is highly monopolized with the top five companies controlling about a third of the market. The drug companies' profits last year totalled a record £353 million, nearly twice the amount spent on new hospital buildings and more than half the annual N H S wage bill. This is where the real poverty of our health service lies.

Adding to the burden on the N H S is the peculiar use of private beds in hospitals. Only one in 100 beds is officially private, yet consultants spend a sixth of their time on private work. The reason they do so is obvious: it pays more for a consultant to look after rich patients in private beds than to tend to the general run of humanity in the general beds. A consultant can earn more in four hours' private work than a nurse gets in a year.

Who pays for welfare?

We are usually told by the press and on television that welfare benefits are paid for out of taxation on the rich for the benefit of the poor. It is nonsense. 'The British tax system is on the whole a non-progressive one', writes Kincaid in his well-informed book, *Poverty and Equality in Britain.* The bare bones of the system are illustrated in the following table taken from the book (p. 108). It refers to only one family size, namely two adults and three children. It shows that the progressive effects of income tax are virtually nullified by the fact that the other main forms of taxation take a much higher proportion of low incomes than of high incomes.

Proportion of income taken by major taxes
1969: households of 2 adults, 3 children

Weekly income	Income tax per cent	National insurance per cent	Expenditure taxes & rates per cent
£16-19	–	4.0	24.2
£23-28	7.0	4.0	18.8
£60 and over	17.0	1.0	12.6

The overall result is that there is very little difference in the percentage of income paid in all forms of taxation between high and low income households. And that is enough to blow up the widely accepted theory that in Britain the tax system is progressive, ie. the higher the income the higher the *rate* of taxation.

The future

Whenever economic growth has been slow, and accompanied by balance of payments difficulties, one of the first casualties has been the social services.

In November 1964 the first Budget of the new Wilson government was announced. It included increases in social benefits. But, as Wilson wrote after the event,

We were soon to learn that decisions on pensions and taxation were no longer to be regarded, as in the past, as decisions for parliament alone. The combination of tax increases with increased social security benefits provoked the first of a series of attacks on sterling, by speculators and others, which beset almost every action of the government for the next five years.

(H. Wilson, *The Labour Government 1964-70,* Penguin, 1974, p.57)

Especially insistent on a cut in the social services was the Governor of the Bank of England, Lord Cromer. Wilson reports:

We had to listen night after night to demands that there should be immediate cuts in government expenditure, and particularly in those parts of government expenditure which related to the social services. It was not long before we were being asked, almost at pistol-point, to cut back on expenditure, even to the point of stopping the road-building programme, or schools which were only half constructed.

(Wilson, pp. 61-62)

The run on the pound continued. But on 25 November

In the afternoon when I was addressing a meeting for the Freedom from Hunger Campaign at Church House, I received a message that the Governor had successfully raised $3,000 million from the central bankers. He had done a magnificent job. Heaven knows what he said about my possible intentions on the international telephone as he explained the alternatives. I did not inquire.

(Wilson, p. 66)

Since we are unable to tap Lord Cromer's telephone — unlike our rulers who can tap ours almost at will — we have to guess what the Hon. Lord did say on the phone. Could it have been that the raising of pensions would be postponed until March the following year? And meanwhile, please God, the number of old age pensioners would be seriously cut down by a bad winter, while inflation would eat into the real value of the pensions promise.

On 16 January 1968 Wilson announced that, faced with the increasing balance of payments trouble, he had no alternative but to carry out harsh cuts in the social services.

> On education, I announced the 'difficult, not to say repugnant'
> decision to defer from 1971 until 1973 the raising of the school
> leaving age to 16 ... Free milk in secondary schools – this was
> another emotive issue – was to stop ... we announced the rein-
> troduction of the prescription charges at 2s 6d per item ...
> Dental treatment charges were raised from £1 to 30s.
>
> (Wilson, pp. 614-15)

Some Labour leaders went so far as to invent a theory to justify the imposition of this increasing burden on the people instead of on the rich. Richard Crossman argued:

> We should not be afraid to look for alternative sources of
> revenue less dependent on the Chancellor's whims ... I should
> not rule out obtaining a higher proportion of the cost of the
> service from the health service contribution.
>
> (R. H. S. Crossman, *Paying for the Social Services,* Fabian
> Society, London, 1969)

Crossman's argument naturally opened the door to Sir Keith Joseph, the Tory who followed him as Secretary of the Social Services. Joseph naturally went further:

> 'Increased dental charges announded in October would give a
> financial incentive to patients to look after their teeth', he said.
> They would, therefore, have a 'beneficial effect on dental
> health'.
>
> (*Guardian,* 3 February 1971)

By the same token, if burial charges were raised fewer people would choose to die!

In the coming couple of years the British balance of payments will be four or five times deeper in the red than in 1964 or 1968, and economic growth will be slower than in the earlier period, or even negative. In the circumstances there can be no doubt that the attack on the social services will be worse under the present Wilson government than under the last one.

The first services to be axed will be those provided by

local authorities. Pressed by the financial squeeze and more or less immune from organized local pressure, they are almost bound to skimp on housing, education, and the other services they provide.

Already a number of local authorities are finding themselves in difficulty. 'The London Borough of Richmond, already £2 million into the red with half of its financial year gone, is by no means untypical', reported the *Sunday Times* (13 October 1974).

A week later the same paper reported in an article entitled 'How the Old and Sick will Suffer':

Many directors of social services are now forecasting closure of some homes for old people and children before 1975 is out. Help for disabled people is jeopardized as well, despite being a statutory duty for local authorities.

Home helps and meals on wheels services for the elderly could also be in danger. Yet local authorities face the dilemma that cuts in the help which enables old people to stay in their own homes may lead to increased financial commitment, because these old people might then have to be put in sheltered residential accommodation, at possibly an even greater cost.

Among the local government economies under consideration social services are particularly vulnerable . . .

The extent of the problems arising from local government's lack of cash is illustrated by the threat to the disabled. The Chronically Sick and Disabled Persons Act, sponsored by Alf Morris in 1970, made it mandatory for local authorities to provide many aids and services to disabled and mentally handicapped people.

But several local authorities now say that some of the provisions under this Act, such as telephones, holidays and house adaptations, would have to be among the first facilities axed to ensure that other services, including meals on wheels, and home helps, may be continued.

What is to be done?

A docker's wife wrote a marvellous letter:

After trying for ten years 'officially' to get these [thalidomide] kids some money, without success, it's about time that some-

thing was done 'unofficially'. I am surprised that dockers have
not done something about blacking Distillers' products, which I
am sure are exported through some docks in the country.
(*Dockworker*, December 1972)

She was absolutely right. The dockers who freed The Five
had the industrial power to force Distillers to cough up
money for those unfortunate children.

The history of the British labour movement shows
clearly how industrial action can defend the social services
or even improve them. It was, after all, the Liberal government's response to a tide of exceptional industrial militancy
that laid the foundations of the modern welfare state. It
was a rent strike backed by the industrial action of
engineering workers in Glasgow that made Lloyd George
introduce a Rent Act for the whole country in 1915. In
November 1921 the National Unemployed Workers' Movement forced through one of the most important improvements: the payment of supplements to the basic unemployment benefit for men with families.

We are entering into a period of mass aggressive action
by working people. Properly led, politically mobilized, that
action at the point of production can be of immense help
to working people and their relatives, the old and sick, the
housewife and the child.

We have already seen some solidarity action of this kind.
Manchester dockers struck in support of the nurses during
their pay dispute last autumn. Four thousand workers
came out in solidarity with the nurses at C. A. Parsons,
Newcastle; four miners' lodges came out on a 24-hour strike
in the same cause in South Wales. On 22 November 1972,
6,000 construction workers on the Anchor Site, Scunthorpe,
struck in support of higher pensions.

It is not enough. We need to learn from Italy where
there have been major strikes over housing and pensions.
One report from there ran:

Socialist Worker, 29 September 1973

Workers' committees are now sitting down planning a campaign to refuse to pay rents which are more than 10 per cent of monthly wage packets. And a bizarre protest at rising bus fares is the latest worker move to win substantial support.

For the past two weeks thousands of commuting factory workers in the bleak industrial hinterlands of Milan and Turin have been flatly refusing to pay recent bus fare increases. Faced with galloping inflation and growing unemployment, they are insisting on paying the former rates.

The technique is perfectly simple and is now beginning to be imitated throughout the north and as far south as Naples. Commuters appoint a bus delegate to collect their 'self-reduced' fares, which are then accumulated and paid by weekly postal order to the bus companies.

The campaign has already had results. In some cases companies refused to carry the protestors. The result, foreseen by the organizers, was that factories were paralyzed. In these cases factory managements themselves successfully exerted pressure on the bus companies to reduce fares to pre-increase levels.

(*Sunday Times,* 13 October 1974)

Another report tells about a trade union campaign against electricity rises:

After finding that a massive increase in the price of electricity was going to fall mainly on home consumers, the electrical union called on them to pay only half their next bill.

In Turin, 13,000 families have already sent the national electricity company a form which declares: 'As instructed by the union movement we are paying only half our next electricity bill'.

(*Socialist Worker,* 19 October 1974)

Another report: the *Guardian* of 21 October 1974 states:

Left-wing demonstrators yesterday took over two supermarkets in Milan, occupying the checkout points for about 30 minutes, and charging their companions and other customers all goods at half price. (The owners complained that they lost £3,000 during this half-hour.)

6.
The Call for a Strong State

As the crisis deepens, and the old prescriptions like incomes policy or unemployment prove to be inadequate, some members of the ruling class feel the need to reach out for total solutions on the far right.

Lurching to the right

Geoffrey Rippon's call for a 'Citizens' Voluntary Reserve, is one such reaction. In his words:

> ... at a time when the foundations of our society are being shaken by violence and extremism we must take steps to ensure the maintenance of order. A Conservative government must provide for an adequate level of reserves and for the strengthening of the Territorials, and strengthen the police and create a Citizens' Voluntary Reserve for home defence and duties in aid of the civil power.

(*Observer,* 8 September 1974)

In the same spirit a group of Conservative M Ps — Harold Gurden (Birmingham Selly Oak), Mrs Jill Knight (Birmingham Edgbaston), Carol Mather (Esher), Angus Maude (Stratford), Airey Neave (Abingdon), and Norman Tebbit (Chingford) — wrote to Mr Heath and the Shadow Home Secretary, Sir Keith Joseph, advocating a force of volunteers to aid the police. Even further to the right is Colonel David Stirling, founder of the British army's S A S units, and boss of G B 75, the secret volunteer scabbing organization being trained to take over factories, power stations, and essential services in the event of a general strike. Also in this group is Unison, led by General Sir Walter Walker, formerly a commander in N A T O.

Sir Keith Joseph and Geoffrey
Rippon: A recent portrait.

Socialist Worker, 14 September 1974

Cold water from Major General Clutterbuck

The call for private armies is not without its critics in the ruling class. One of the first was Major General Clutterbuck, who argued convincingly that 'proposals for private volunteer forces to man public services in an emergency are both futile and dangerous'. Clutterbuck's arguments are persuasive, and clearly represent the mainstream of ruling-class opinion:

Pouring 100,000 of General Sir Walter Walker's and Colonel David Stirling's volunteers into the power stations, pumping stations, transport depots and docks in a time of national crisis would achieve less than nothing, if it drove another million (or conceivably ten million) out of the other gate.

General Walker's Unison volunteers – with or without government approval – could not hope to do the work of even a small section of the 10,000 dockers, for instance, still less that of the 100,000 power station men. Of course, they know this and would aim only to man a small and vital element. But even this could be quickly defeated by the union members sitting-in or going slow or merely mounting strong picket lines.

In any case, very few public utilities are labour intensive. The Post Office, refuse collection and transport provide about the only exceptions. All the others depend ultimately on a number of skilled men, small in relation to the total labour force, but large in relation to any conceivable volunteer force. Amateurs, even 'trained' amateurs, could never be put in charge of dock cranes or railway engines. The idea of anyone but a professional being at large in the control room of a power station is a truly terrifying prospect, even if he were under the supervision of the managerial staff who may be expected to stay at their posts – and even they might not do so in such circumstances. If General Walker plans to recruit skilled men who are already in the industry, in the hope that they will act as blacklegs, he grossly underestimates the strength of collective loyalty among trade union members.

In any case, servicemen could do little more than that because their numbers – especially of skilled men – are too small. There could never be any question of the army being able to run essential services for a big city, such as London or Belfast. And the last thing you should do with soldiers is to launch them on to a task which is obviously beyond their powers. That was why the decision was taken — quite rightly — not to use the army to try to break the Ulster Workers' Council general strike last May.

Neither military nor volunteer labour can ever break a general strike, though they could easily provoke one. General Walker is God's gift to all militants.

(*Observer,* 22 September 1974)

If the British army finds it difficult to run four power stations in Northern Ireland, how will it manage to run 200 power stations in Britain . . . and the docks . . . and the mines . . .?

Appeasement has the upper hand

Every politican needs to learn the lesson from scratch: you can't take on the whole labour movement and hope to win.

Harold Wilson learned it during the rebellion of the lower paid in 1969, when he tried — and failed — to get the trade unions to accept 'In Place of Strife', the bosses' charter. Since then he hasn't moved a step out of line with the trade union leaders.

Then there is Heath, 'Selsdon Man', challenger of the miners, jailer of the dockers, architect of Phases One, Two and Three. He learned the same lesson in his final confrontation with the miners. He too has made his U-turn towards appeasement and moderation.

Business knew it all along. Very few employers resorted to the hated National Industrial Relations Court during the whole of its existence. The big ones — I C I, Leyland, Ford — would not touch it. The reasons were obvious even before the Industrial Relations Act became law, and were pointed out by the representative of the Shipbuilding Employers' Federation in evidence to the Donovan Commission:

I do not see how you are going to make a sanction work. You just cannot put 5,000 strikers in jail and if you fine them and they do not pay the fine, what are you going to do? I do not see how this would work out in practice, unless everyone observed the law voluntarily. If people kick over the traces in large numbers, the law is helpless . . . .

In the end the Industrial Relations Act was smashed by working-class action in defence of the Pentonville Five in what *Socialist Worker* called 'the greatest victory for the British working class for more than half a century'. Its original aim — to reduce the power of rank and file workers to withstand the employers' offensive — had failed. By July 1974, when it was repealed, there were no mourners. Even the *Financial Times* remarked: 'Few will regret the death of the Tory Law.'

New policies were clearly needed. As *Socialist Worker* commented in its editorial 'Exit Stick, Enter Carrot',

Coercion failed. Perhaps guile will succeed in the endless struggle to paralyze the working class. Harold Wilson, Ted Heath and Len Murray are allied together to try it. The Industrial Relations Act is dead. Long live the 'social contract'. That is what the bosses and their agents in the workers' movement are thinking now. (27 July 1974)

If mass strikes, or even general strikes, grow . . .

Events during the 1926 General Strike suggest that the policy of collaborating with the trade union bureaucrats can survive the most massive of mass strikes, without giving way to the extremes promoted by G B 75, Unison, or the fascists.

In September 1925 a new body — the Organization for the Maintenance of Supplies — was announced in the press. It declared:

Numerous suggestions have been made from various quarters for organizing those citizens who would be prepared to volunteer to maintain supplies and vital services in the event of a general strike. It seems, therefore, that the moment has come to announce publicly that such an organization has already been constituted and is at work in many metropolitan boroughs, while steps are being taken to create corresponding organizations in all the principal centres of the kingdom.

(C. Farman, *The General Strike, May 1926*, Panther, 1972, p. 60)

When the General Strike broke out, the number of members in the O M S was some 100,000. Farman tells us:

The great bulk lived in the south and east of England, the largest single number – over 7,000 – being provided by the City of Westminster. The whole of Leeds, for instance, provided only 400 and there were none at all registered in Manchester or Liverpool. During the months preceding the strike the O M S managed to provide discreet training for a limited number of volunteer drivers, telegraph operators and telephonists. But the total of skilled personnel handed over on 3 May was far from impressive. It included 1,322 lorry drivers and 250 Ford van drivers for the G P O trained in O M S 'schools' – usually the testing grounds of private factories – 144 bus drivers, 1,345 car drivers, 640 railway operatives, 166 workers for inland waterways, 91 tramwaymen, and 351 mechanics. There were also 1,194 skilled, semi-skilled and unskilled engineers for the electricity commission. The government itself issued an appeal for volunteers on Sunday evening and recruiting stations were opened the following morning. The sight of continual queues at the London enrolment centre, a temporary wooden hutment erected in the Foreign Office quadrangle in Whitehall, may have seemed impressive, but by 4 May only 6,000 volunteers had come forward and throughout the country the total was no more than 30,000.

(pp. 149-50)

The scabs were not very effective. Although helped by blackleg staff, they could not keep public transport going.

Passenger service on the L M S was 3.8 per cent of normal on 5 May and freight service only 1 per cent of normal; on the L N E R the equivalent figures were 3.4 and 2.2 per cent, and on the Great Western 3.7 and 5 per cent.

On the London Underground 15 out of 315 trains ran on the first day of the strike and these covered short distances only. Of London's 4,400 buses, 300 were running with volunteer crews on Tuesday but the number was down to 40 by the end of the week.

(p. 151)

After the General Strike the future of the O M S came up for discussion:

> The organization, which wanted to secure a permanent status for itself, suggested to the Home Secretary that it should be allowed to maintain an up-to-date file of volunteers for use in future emergencies and that a public appeal should be launched for funds.

However, in a memorandum from the Permanent Under-Secretary to the Home Office,

> John Anderson firmly quashed both suggestions. This argued that a public appeal for funds would be politically divisive at a time when the Prime Minister himself was appealing for unity and tolerance, and that O M S assistance had, anyway, been of 'comparatively small importance'.
>
> (p. 305)

The fascists were even less effective.

> Membership of the British Fascists, set up in 1923, and of the National Fascisti, a militant but minute splinter group of the parent body, numbered only a few thousand . . . neither had any kind of base in the trade unions or popular support outside.

By May 1926

> the British Fascists had virtually ceased to exist as a separate body. When the O M S was launched, a majority of the party's leadership proclaimed that 'at the present moment effective assistance to the state can best be given in seconding the efforts of the O M S'. They withdrew from the British Fascists to form the Loyalists, which as a 'non-political' group was then incorporated into the O M S.
>
> (pp. 62-63)

There were also 'specials' recruited by the government to back up the regular police:

> For scores of thousands of specials there was little to do but ride as escort on the occasional bus or lorry or wander about the streets in police caps and plus fours. On Sunday Fyfe observed that 'The specials are becoming a joke, even among people who

are on the side of the Cabinet. It is so obvious there is nothing for them to do. What did those who made such desperate efforts to enrol them think there would be for them to do?'
(p. 242)

The government won. It did break the strike, but not thanks to the O M S, the fascists or the 'specials'. It won thanks to the General Council of the T U C.

For the ruling class in the coming period the role of the trade union bureaucracy is central, and for the workers it should be so too.

Against sidetracking

There is an extreme right, and it is becoming noisy. It has to be smashed. We should never tolerate people who admit that 'we're busy forming a well-oiled Nazi machine throughout the country' (Martin Webster, National Activities Organizer of the National Front, quoted in the *People*, 9 September 1962), or who state that 'Mein Kampf is my doctrine' (John Tyndall, chairman of the National Front, quoted in the *Guardian*, 8 February 1964). They have to be driven physically from the streets, for fascist movements disintegrate when they can no longer march. But they are not the main enemy. The extreme right is weaker now than in 1926. Then the students manned the trams, and many white-collar workers acted as scabs. Today students are far more radical, while white-collar trade unionism has engulfed hundreds of thousands of people. Above all, industrial workers are now much more confident and assertive than they were in the twenties.

The strategic question for workers is not 'fashy-bashing'. Rather it is how to deal with the trade union bureaucracy who collaborate with the employers; how to create a rank and file movement to act independently of the bureaucracy in defence of wages and conditions; and how to deal with the increasing daily harassments from the state machine.

We shall take up the first two questions in the next

chapter. Now we turn to the activities of the state machine
— the police, the army and the courts.

The Special Patrol Group

The S P G was founded in 1965 under the Labour government. It was a 110-man detachment of specially trained, 'go
anywhere, any time' police. Little attention was paid to
them until the summer of 1972, when they burst into
action against London dockers and printworkers, but there
is little doubt that they were formed under the influence of
American police thinking and with a distinct political
purpose in mind.

Since their first outings against the working-class movement, the S P G in London has doubled to an admitted
strength of 220. Parallel developments have been going on
outside London. The *Sunday Times* reported in January
1974 that in Yorkshire alone there was a special squad of
800 trained police on permanent standby during the
miners' strike.

> A special unit kept watch on known extremists in such areas as
> Stainforth, near the Hatfield Main Colliery, and Cadeby, near
> Mexborough. Gregory (the chief constable) says that he has
> identified possible trouble areas and a plan of action has been
> worked out.

There has also been a trend to integrate police and army
operations. Brigadier Brian Watkins, of the Army General
Staff, explained why:

> The whole period of the miners' strike has made us realize that
> the present size of the police force is too small. It is based on the
> fundamental philosophy that we are a law-abiding country. But
> things have now got to the state where there are not enough
> resources to deal with the increasing numbers who are not
> prepared to respect the law.
> (*The Times,* 23 May 1972)

The election of a Labour government has made no

100

difference to the 'rationalization' going on in both police and army. They are getting themselves ready to deal with 'dissent' on a bigger and bigger scale. Many more policemen are following John Gerrard, founder of the S P G, to the classrooms of the American Military Police School in Atlanta, Georgia, where they learn the tactics that culminated in Red Lion Square.

The secret police

From the very earliest days trade unionists have been closely watched by police spies. They still are and the political leaders who pretend to represent them still see nothing wrong in it. They even use spies against their supporters. Harold Wilson, for example. He writes of the 1966 seamen's strike leaders, Joseph Kenny and James Slater, that they

> live in Liverpool and South Shields respectively and over the past few weeks, when attending the Executive Council in London, they have stayed at the same flat as Mr Jack Coward. Of course, they are free to stay where they like, but Mr Ramelson has visited the flat when they were there and Mr Norris has been in constant touch with them. They have been in continual contact with Mr Ramelson and Mr Norris.
>
> (H. Wilson, *The Labour Government 1964-70,* Penguin, 1971, p. 311)

How did Wilson know? He makes it clear by:

> I decided to make all the facts available to him [Heath] on Privy Counsellor terms, and for good measure to bring to our meeting their senior people responsible for these matters, and one of the operators 'in the field'.

Governments change, but the spying, harassment and 'red-baiting' of militants goes on. The *Sunday Times* reports:

> The Special Branch has been in contact with Strachans since August last year ... and has maintained its interest throughout

101

the sit-in, which began four weeks ago after the firm announced that its two engineering plants at Eastleigh and Hamble, seven miles away, are to close.

(14 April 1974)

So the secret police started their industrial espionage under Tory Home Secretary Robert Carr, and continued it under Labour Home Secretary Roy Jenkins.

The political group identified by the police were the International Socialists. The I S has a local branch in Portsmouth which has been distributing literature to the men sitting-in on how to claim maximum social security benefits.

(*Sunday Times,* 14 April 1974)

How shocking! Advising workers how to go about claiming benefits to which they are entitled! As a matter of fact the I S branch went even further: they actually held collections of money to support the workers sitting-in. Nor is Strachans an isolated case. 'Special Branch sources in London', told the *Daily Telegraph* that

such investigations throughout the country were not unusual. They constituted an important part of detectives' work . . .

(15 April 1974)

And what was the reaction of the T U C to this snooping? An unnamed 'T U C spokesman' is quoted by the *Daily Telegraph* as saying

Understandably, the authorities have to take an interest in anybody likely to be guilty of violence or insurrection. Consequently they are entitled to use all resources available to collect information.

The uniformed police

A major part of their duties is to defend scabs and break strikes. A major part of their training is directed at isolating them from all contact with the labour movement. They are segregated; they are forbidden to take part in active politics or to join a genuine trade union.

102

The Police Act of 1919 makes it illegal for the police to belong to a trade union or association having the object of influencing the pay, pensions or service conditions of any police force. Representations on these matters can only be made through the Police Federation, whose constitution is prescribed in detail in the Act. Every police officer, other than those holding the rank of superintendent and above, automatically belongs to the Federation. Meetings take place in official time and at official expense; and all officials of the Federation must be policemen who are subject to discipline. It is a disciplinary offence, punishable by dismissal from the force, if a policeman 'calls or attends any unauthorized meeting to discuss any matter concerning the force'.

(Police (Discipline) Regulations, 1952, para 6 (h))

One of Wilson's proudest achievements was an increase in the number of policemen during his first administration and an improvement in their equipment. He told the House of Commons:

When the government which I head came to power there were 80,700 police officers in this country. At the end of 1969 the figure was 91,762. At the end of 1964 the number of civilians employed in the police service was 18,200. They now total 33,000. And every one of them either makes the policeman more effective or, more directly, releases a policeman to do a police job . . .

In the last full year before the present administration took office, the total annual expenditure on equipping the police was running at about £5½ million. Today we are spending £12 million . . . Twice as many police cars are now equipped with radio. Against 500 personal radio sets for two-way communication 5½ years ago there are now about 23,000 pocket radio sets of an improved design, an increase of 4,500 per cent . . .

(Quoted in Wilson, pp. 971-72)

The army

Sir Charles Napier, who commanded the Northern District at the height of the Chartist movement from 1839 to 1841, drew the conclusion regarding the use of troops which has been followed by British governments ever since:

> I say the government must have a strong body of police with paid magistrates, to uphold the law without calling for troops on every occasion: *the soldier forms the reserve and should not be the advanced guard.*
>
> (Quoted in J. Harvey and K. Hood, *The British State,* London, 1958, p. 132)

The British army has a rich history of strike-breaking at home.

> In 1910 [troops] were sent to Tonypandy valley on the orders of Mr Winston Churchill to provide protection for imported blackleg labour during the miners' strike; in 1911, when the great railway strike broke out, 'practically the whole of the troops in Great Britain were on duty scattered along the railway system'; in the railway strike of 1919 there was again a great display of military force. During the General Strike of 1926, though the ruling class relied mainly on the police and special constables to protect blacklegs, troops were continuously held in readiness, and were used to convoy food from the docks to Hyde Park, while warships landed supplies at Liverpool.
>
> Since the Second World War the armed forces have again been frequently used to defeat strikes. On this front there has, however, been one significant change. Formerly troops were always used for the *protection* of civilian blacklegs, but since the war they have been used repeatedly as *blacklegs themselves.* During the period of the [Attlee] government, the navy was used once and the army on no less than nine separate occasions for this purpose.
>
> (Harvey and Hood, pp. 111-12)

The command structure in capitalist society is carried to extremes in its armed forces. High army offices are recruited from the ruling class. Out of 112 top commanders in the army 82, or 73 per cent, were former public school boys (*Army List,* Spring 1973, and *Who's Who,* 1973). Out of 17 admirals and vice-admirals, 15 went to public schools (Labour Research Department, *Two Nations,* p. 27).

The main route to a commission is the Royal Military Academy at Sandhurst.

The Times tells us that:

Use of troops as strike-breakers under the Labour government 1945-50

8 April 1946: 600 Smithfield provision workers struck. Troops were sent on 15 April, when 3,000 meatporters struck in sympathy.

8 January 1947: great road haulage strike numbering over 20,000, including 400 Smithfield drivers. Troops sent into Smithfield on 13 January, whereupon all meat and provision workers came out in sympathy.

15 March 1948: 1,300 Ministry of Works employees — engineers, attendants, boilermen, liftmen, etc — struck in protest at delay in settling wage claim. On 18 March troops were sent to stoke boilers at Buckingham Palace, whereupon shop stewards decided to call out all engineering grades if troops were not withdrawn.

14 June 1948: London Dock Strike, which later spread to the Mersey, involving some 30,000; on 23 June troops brought in to handle perishable food.

14 May 1949: Avonmouth Dockers refused to unload a Canadian ship manned by the International Seafarers' Union, which was blacklegging on the official Canadian seamen's union. On 27 May troops unloaded a banana ship, following which crane drivers refused to work with troops; on 2 June troops began to unload all ships, following which British seamen struck against troops used on lock-gates, etc. Later, troops moved into the London docks, whereupon workers in haulage firms and in Spitalfield refused to handle goods unloaded by troops.

16 September 1949: Belfast power station strike; troops drafted in immediately.

12 December 1949: 1,000 struck at three London power stations. Troops were semt in, whereupon a further 1,600 at Barking power station came out in protest.

19 April 1950: London dock strike against expulsions of leaders from TGWU for solidarity with Canadian seamen: 9,000 came out. On 24 April troops were moved in and a further 4,500 promptly came out.

24 June 1950: 1,200 Smithfield meat drivers struck in protest at delay in settling claim. Troops drafted in, and 900 meat porters struck in protest.

1 September 1950: strike of London gas maintenance workers started and spread to 15 gasworks in the North Thames Gas Board area; on 3 October, 100 naval ratings left Chatham Barracks to start taking over the maintenance work at gas-works.

(Harvey and Hood, p.112)

105

The schools which have sent most cadets to the R M A since the war are broadly those which served it best before 1939, when 180 schools still exercized a near monopoly and the breeding of officer-cadets was regarded, rightly or wrongly, as the special privilege of public schools.

(4 February 1953, quoted in Harvey and Hood, p. 114)

'Breeding' is central to military promotion prospects. To quote Sir John Slessor, Chief of the Air Staff, 1950-52:

It is unfashionable nowadays to talk about an officer class. I have yet to hear anyone deny that breeding and training are of some importance in horses if one wants to produce winners, but in some quarters it seems to be considered a solecism to suggest the same thing may apply to men . . . if we believe in the public school system, if we continue to claim its privileges, let us have the courage to admit that it does – and I believe, always will – produce the great majority of the best leaders of men in Britain.

(Quoted in Harvey and Hood, p. 115)

To insulate the army from the labour movement, soldiers are not allowed to involve themselves in any political activity. As Churchill put it in a letter to the Secretary of State for War on 17 October 1941:

I do not approve of this system of encouraging political discussion in the army among soldiers as such . . . There cannot be controversy without prejudice to discipline. The only sound principle is 'No politics in the army.'

(Quoted in Harvey and Hood, p. 117)

The courts and the Civil Service

The courts, and the Civil Service generally, are accessories to the police and the army. Their top officials are recruited by and large from the capitalist class:

In 1973, out of 103 High Court judges, 83 came from public schools, 87 went to Oxford or Cambridge (from *The Law List, 1973, Who's Who, 1973,* and *Public and Prepatory Schools Year Book, 1973*).

Of the 23 top jobs in the Foreign and Commonwealth Office (permanent under-secretaries, deputy under-secretaries, assistant under-secretaries) at least 15 (or 65 per cent) were educated at public schools and 19 out of the 23 went to Oxford or Cambridge.

The latest comprehensive investigation into the social background of the administrative Civil Service was done for the Fulton Committee on the Civil Service and published in 1969. As summed up by Lord Fulton, chairman of the committee, the survey showed that:

> 79 per cent of direct recruits into the top echelons of the service were of upper and middle-class backgrounds . . . 56 per cent of the top administrators were educated at fee-paying schools, and two-thirds came from Oxford and Cambridge.
>
> (*The Times*, 7 May 1969, quoted in Labour Research Department, *Two Nations*, p. 27)

The persecution of militants and revolutionaries

While there is no danger of a fascist or extreme right wing take-over in the foreseeable future, nor even of massive police and army mobilization against strikes, there is a danger of more and more police spying on trade unionists and revolutionary socialists. The rough part of the state machine – the narks and the Special Patrol Group – will have more work to do.

For while it is true that the General Council of the T U C was the main weapon of the employing class in 1926, the mass arrest of Communists was still quite handy. Altogether some 1,200 Communists were arrested – about a quarter of all party members! Their offence? In most cases possession of a 'document containing any report or statement . . . likely to cause disaffection . . . among the civilian population'. In other words, printing or distributing strike bulletins.

The recent heavy financial punishment of *Socialist*

Socialist Worker, 26 August 1972

Worker by the High Court is a warning of what we might expect.

What should the working class do about the state machine?

Marx and Lenin argued that the bureaucratic, hierarchical, capitalist state machine had to be smashed for workers to achieve socialism. In place of this machine a new kind of state has to be built, a democratic workers' state, without a standing army and police, and with no bureaucracy. All officials would be elected by working people. All of them would be recallable at any time. All would get wages no higher than those of the workers who elected them.

Such a state existed for a short time in the Paris Commune of 1871 – the first workers' government in the world.

> The first decree of the Commune ... was the suppression of the standing army, and the substitution for it of the armed people ... The Commune was formed of the municipal councillors,

chosen by universal suffrage in various wards of the town, responsible and revocable at short terms. The majority of its members were naturally working men, or acknowledged representatives of the working class . . . Instead of continuing to be the agent of the central government, the police were at once stripped of their political attributes, and turned into the responsible and at all times revocable agents of the Commune. So were the officials of all other branches of the administration. From the members of the Commune downwards, the public service had to be done at *workmen's wages.* The vested interests and the representation allowances of the high dignitaries of state disappeared along with the high dignitaries themselves . . . The judicial functionaries were to be divested of sham independence . . . Like the rest of the public servants, magistrates and judges were to be elective, responsible and revocable.

(Karl Marx, *The Civil War in France,* London, 1941, pp. 40-41)

In most cases, however, workers who have moved towards a revolutionary situation have not seized the time, have not smashed the state. In all these instances, the working class was itself smashed.

In France in May-June 1936, soon after the election of a Popular Front government, a spontaneous general strike broke out. There followed mass occupations of the factories. The terrified employers offered no resistance. For a moment, they lost confidence. But the leaders of the Socialist and Communist Parties sold out. They accepted a 40-hour week and a general wage rise of 11 per cent. They took concessions within the system and left the system standing. Naturally the ruling class regained its confidence. Its army was intact. It threw everything into the counterattack. Prices rose fast and quickly wiped out the wage rise. Less than two years later the Popular Front government was defeated in a wave of reaction. The new Conservative government scrapped the 40-hour week, raising it to 48 hours. Soon the new government was loving up to Hitler's regime in Germany.

In September 1939, Daladier turned on the Communist Party that had supported him in 1936, banned and hunted it. The party's hand was bitten by the mouth it had so earnestly fed.

Even more dramatic were the occupations of factories in northern Italy in 1920. The entire industrial power of the country was paralyzed by the workers' movement. But state power was not seized, the army was not won, the mass strikes were not extended.

The capitalists, who had been so shaken that some were prepared to hand over the factories and flee the country, regained confidence. They put their faith in a new fascist movement which promised to annihilate the workers' organizations. In 1922, Mussolini marched on Rome to topple the old parliamentary government. His march was supported by the army all the way, and the Italian working class was smashed for more than 20 years.

The recent tragic case of Chile fits the same pattern. The generals were not removed when Allende came to power on a wave of popular support. They did not remain idle, and at the first opportunity wreaked a terrible vengeance on the mass of the people.

The long-term danger of a right-wing, even fascist, counter-revolution

The last miners' strike brought home, as nothing else could, the difficulties facing any government that does not have the support, or at least the acquiescence of the trade union leaders. The ruling class learned that they could not hold down wages by force, that they need to use persuasion. They recognized the need to have Labour in office in the current period.

It is a gamble for them. Wilson is trying to bridge two contradictory aims — to run capitalism more efficiently than the Tories, and at the same time, to preserve working-class electoral support by doling out a few concessions. When he tried to do it last time he lost both the support of the workers — as expressed in the rebellion of the lower paid and in the mass resistance to his version of the Industrial Relations Act ('In Place of Strife') – and the respect of big business; he was too soft towards the unions.

Wilson's problems now are greater. The crisis is so deep that enormous government subsidies will need to go to private industry to keep management happy; immense pressure will have to be put on workers to restrain their claims. But with inflation roaring along, workers' resistance to restraint will be adamant, and many of the ideological ties that bind them to the system will be stretched to breaking point. After all, when workers ask for a few shillings a week in a single shop, the ideological veil covering the system as a whole is not pulled aside, but when 100,000 workers demand a 20 per cent rise to keep up with rising prices the class struggle moves into the centre of the stage.

Labour will fail. It might fail more than once. Each time its methods will be applied with less conviction. Each time the call for strong government to overcome the indecision, to impose order and system, will ring out louder and clearer. Ultimately the demand will be made to smash the unions, for a capitalism that suffers from permanent and deepening crisis is incompatible with trade unionism.

This is not to say that leading sections of the capitalist class are for smashing the unions now. Of course not. For the moment, all we have to expect is that greater use will be made of state violence against the workers – violence more or less within the law. For the moment the employing class can still use the trade union bureaucracy while increasing their use of naked police power, the courts and the army.

But as the crisis deepens they will depend increasingly on the second. Ultimately they will face the stark alternative: either they break the back of workers' organization in the factories, or the workers get rid of them. That will be the day of the fascists.

Capitalism, after all, is not wedded to parliamentary

democracy but to profit. If in the interest of profit parliamentary democracy needs to be smashed, big business will not flinch from doing its duty. In Germany in 1933 it supported Hitler's attack on parliament, the trade unions and democratic rights. In Austria in 1934 it supported Dolfuss. In Italy in 1924, in Spain in 1936, in Greece in 1967, in Chile last year – whenever the left looked as if it might tip the class balance away from capital, big business rushed to overthrow the freedoms they claimed to uphold. There is no reason to believe that in its hour of need the British capitalist class will behave any differently. Already there is the stench of blood to come in the fantasies of Unison and G B 75, in the war cry of the National Front ('The Reds, the Rats, we've got to get rid of the Reds'), in the deaths of the repentant agent Kenneth Lennon and of the young anti-fascist Kevin Gately. Whether the stench spreads or not depends not only on the workers' immediate reaction, but even more on their ability to defend their living standards, to go on the offensive against the employers and the state, to strengthen their self-confidence, raise their class consciousness and organized power.

In conclusion

Within the next few years, as profits and reforms are seen to be more and more incompatible, as the weapon of persuasion fails, which it is bound to do, as the Labour government finds itself unable to satisfy big business and also maintain its popular support, the rulers will increasingly resort to brute force – the law, the police, and finally the army.

In defending themselves from the S P G, from the Special Branch and from their accomplices – the private armies of General Walker and Colonel Stirling or the scabs of the National Front – workers will have to learn in practice what the real function of the state is, and how

112

decisive it is for them to hold state power. For unless they build a new state to achieve socialism, the ruling class will use the present state to break out of the crisis in the only way they know — barbarism, the barbarisms of Hitler and of Hiroshima.

That is why the present struggle of workers has not only immediate relevance, but is decisive in shaping our future.

7.
The Dead Weight of the Trade Union Bureaucracy

Wee fat full-time union official
waistcoat bursting with status
thirty years off the tools
grovels at the bosses' table
looking for a handout
for a dram
to give him strength
to climb on the workers' backs.
*Anon**

1972 was a magnificent year for the British working class. The class struggle rose to new heights in terms of the number of workers involved, in the size and duration of the strikes and, above all, in the quality of the struggle. There were many more large-scale and prolonged strikes in that year than in any of the previous ten. Even if we exclude the miners' strikes, only once in British history was the number of strike days greater — in 1919.

1972 saw the first national miners' strike since 1926, and this time the miners won. It saw the biggest building workers' strike ever, 300,000 out over 12 weeks. The last similar confrontation was in 1923, when the employers locked the builders out.

The quality of the struggle was also very high. There was a purely political strike to free the Pentonville Five. There was a solidarity strike of 50,000 engineers in Birmingham in support of the miners. There were strikes in support of old age pensioners for the first time ever — 6,000 construction workers coming out at the Anchor site near Scunthorpe.

*K. Weller and E. Stanton, *What Happened at Fords?*, London, n.d., p. 6.

That year the rank and file showed its mettle; the bureaucracy only its bankruptcy.

While rank and file miners were picketing power stations, and shaping up to a magnificent victory with the help of railwaymen, lorry drivers and workers in the power industry, their industrial and political leaders did nothing or worse than nothing. Joe Gormley, President of the N U M, declared on the eve of the strike that if the government raised their £2 offer just a little the strike would not take place. (The official union claim was £9, £6 and £5 for face, underground and surface workers.) Harold Lever, Shadow Minister for Fuel and Power, attacked the government for mismanaging the dispute, declaring that if Labour had been in power they would have settled the miners' wage claim for less than the Tories.

Prices were rising very steeply and workers were finding life tough. The Heath government was reeling under the miners' blows. If ever there was a time for the other big battalions of the trade union movement to march forward and put in hefty wage claims, it was then. But the union leaders did nothing of the sort.

The engineers are a case in point.

Hugh Scanlon and the engineers

In August 1971 the Confederation of Shipbuilding and Engineering Unions (C S E U) representing some two million workers, presented a major wage claim to the Engineering Employers' Federation. The claim was for a new skilled minimum rate of £25, a 35-hour week, equal pay, a fourth week's holiday, more lay-off pay, improved overtime and shift premiums, and a substantial wage rise. Talks carried on for several months before it became clear that the employers were not prepared to offer more than a token. The negotiations finally collapsed in January 1972 when the miners' struggle was in full spate. The engineering leaders could have gained a tremendous victory had they called a national strike and allied themselves with the miners. Instead they chose to fight on a plant by plant basis.

'This proved to be a near disaster,' wrote the International Socialists in their pamphlet *The 1973 Engineering Pay Claim*.

> For during the whole of the eight months that passed between the January decision and the signing of the eventual settlement in August 1972, these so-called leaders never once gave a real lead or any fighting direction.

> They never agitated and campaigned for the claim or publicized it or even attempted to mobilize mass support behind it. They never once even seriously discussed the possibility of extending it into a national strike or even sought to direct and supervise that strategy that they themselves were the architects of. They could have selected the most important companies in the EEF and then concentrated their resources in a major effort to try and compel these to concede the claim. But they didn't. They could have led a national overtime ban or a national work to rule or declared an arbitrary 35-hour working week or any combination of these. But they didn't. They could have selected certain key districts, organized mass campaigns of propaganda and support, initiated solidarity action and financial levies in other areas and generally acted as a general staff. But they didn't.

> Indeed not only did they abstain from giving any leadership but many of them frequently behaved in such a manner as to undermine any attempt at a serious fight.

For instance, in February,

> the Sheffield District of the A U E W announced that they intended to organize a city-wide strike of all their 45,000 members. Its leaders said that this would last until such time as the Sheffield District of the E E F conceded the claim . . . instead of welcoming and supporting this first and long overdue expression of militancy, Scanlon and the A U E W Executive instructed the District to abandon its proposals as they were unconstitutional and contrary to that union rule that required a District ballot before a District strike. The Executive had no proposals about how to overcome this hold-up and thereby maintain the District's enthusiasm. Consequently the effect of this intervention not only undermined morale in that area but

also showed that the union leaders were not in favour of the most effective and decisive fight for the claim. Instead they were determined to rigidly confine it to the inevitably doomed factory by factory strategy.

The final bankruptcy of the leadership showed itself during the Manchester District campaign.

This turned out to be the only area where a large-scale battle was organized in support of the claim. After six weeks when more than 30 different factories were on strike or had been occupied, Scanlon finally visited the area but only to tell a special shop stewards' meeting that settlements could be negotiated which excluded a reduction in hours.

The leadership in Manchester, wrote another commentator,

never called regular meetings of shop stewards, refused to organize delegations to visit other areas, and ignored several calls for meetings and co-ordination between representatives of the occupied workplaces. They never led any marches or demonstrations in support of the claim and so totally failed to mobilize large numbers of rank and file engineers.

Instead of using the sit-ins as organizing bases that involved thousands of workers who could then be directed to picket anywhere in the area, the Manchester campaign allowed them to disperse and contribute very little.

(R. Rosewell in *International Socialism*, no 53, October-December 1972)

And so after nine months of a miserably led campaign the unions capitulated and an agreement was signed. It was so bad for the workers that

the director of the Shipbuilding Employers' Federation was able to delightedly state, 'The settlement, being an increase in basic minimum rates and not a general increase, affected only a comparatively small number of employees . . . the total cost of the settlement to the industry is in percentage terms substantially below what is generally understood as being the government's norm at the present time'.

(*The 1973 Engineering Pay Claim*)

The settlement was worth less than half the miners' rise,

and only two-thirds of what the railwaymen got a few months earlier. It succeeded in raising the minimum rate to £25 spread over two payments, and gained two days' extra holidays. But there was no reduction in hours, or general wage rise, or any other concession. Instead of lasting for a year, it lasted effectively 20 months, because eight months were consumed in getting it.

And imagine, all this took place in August 1972 – six months after the miners' victory and a month after the fantastic success of the working class in freeing the Pentonville Five!

The second round of engineering claims came just in the middle of the second national miners' strike. Again Scanlon managed to snatch defeat out of the jaws of victory.

On 2 December 1973, at a meeting of engineering workers at Luton, he argued against approaches being made at a national level to consider joint action between the miners and the engineers. In the New Year, prompted by the 'left', the A U E W leadership decided on an overtime ban. There was one drawback though: Heath plunged the engineering industry into a two-day lockout as part of his strategy for beating the miners. Under the circumstances an overtime ban was pure nonsense. So the A U E W leadership decided to postpone all action until after the miners' strike!

On 13 January 1974, Scanlon went as far as to say, on I T V's *Weekend World,* that all he was after was 'an offer to the limit of Phase Three, not to break it'. This was serious news. It meant he was determined to leave the miners on their own. It also meant that he was willing to sell his own members out as well, for the engineers' claim went far beyond Phase Three. It was for a £10 rise on basic rates, equal pay, a 35-hour week, and four weeks' annual holiday.

In the event the sell-out was even worse than intended. It ended with the engineers getting a 2-2½ per cent rise even though Phase Three allowed for 7 per cent.

Jack Jones and the dockers

The contrast between the militancy of the rank and file and the bankruptcy of the leadership appeared even starker, if that is possible, in the case of the dockers, when they came out to free The Five from Pentonville. The strike was unofficial. Jack Jones did nothing. He kept his mouth shut even after Reg Prentice, Shadow Minister of Labour, attacked The Five for breaking the law, and for seeking self-advertisement. It was only after the rank and file dockers developed an independent movement of their own that Jack Jones decided to speak up and propose an official one-day strike, for, as he warned his colleagues, 'if the General Council did not . . . unofficial bodies would assume leadership'.

Once The Five were freed and the government had capitulated to the threat of a spontaneous general strike, Jack Jones decided to throw his weight and that of the union on the side of the dockers in their fight for job security. An official strike was called.

If 41,000 dockers could win an unofficial strike, the support of a union of 1,700,000 should surely have won them the official one. But no. The mass of the members were left out of it. Only a few hundred militants picketed open ports. No mass demonstrations were held. The union did not call on their own lorry driver members, let alone on the N U R and A S L E F, to black goods coming through scab ports. The strike was prolonged artificially to tire the dockers — the final draft of the revised Jones-Aldington Agreement which ended the dispute was ready at least one week before it was published. Even the timing of the mass meetings was arranged so as to isolate and defeat the militants, with Tilbury voting before London and Hull.

The Jones-Aldington Agreement, it was said, promised job security to the dockers. Jack Jones did not, of course, tell the dockers who Lord Aldington was. How many knew that he was once a deputy chairman of the Tory Party? How many knew that, as vice-chairman of G E C, he had presided over the sacking of 50,000 workers? Above all, how many dockers knew of the secret survey undertaken by the National Ports Council, that projected a decline in the number of registered dockers from 41,000 in 1972 to less than 30,000 in 1975, with losses of 5,000 jobs in London, a similar number in Liverpool, and approximately 1,500 in Hull, Grimsby, Immingham, Bristol and the small Lancashire ports? The bitter fruits of the sell-out matured quickly. Within a year Laurie Flynn reported:

> The so-called concessions in the Jones-Aldington Report have never been implemented. And the employers have simply received a massive amount of public money to get rid of a record number of registered dockers in the shortest possible period.
>
> By February, when the specially boosted severance payments were brought to an end, 9,000 men who last summer had been willing to fight for job security, and to take on the Industrial Relations Act, had been persuaded to pack it in. There are now only 32,000 registered dockers left in the industry.
>
> ('Nine Thousand Docks Jobs Go Down the River', *Socialist Worker*, 4 August 1973)

The two souls of the trade union bureaucracy

In the last few years, every time the Tory government was sent reeling by some section of the working class, the trade union bureaucracy has rushed forward to prop it up.

It is hardly by chance. Trade union officialdom is caught in a contradictory position. Their trade unions are organizations for the defence of workers against the employers; but they themselves live completely differently and separately from the workers they represent. Even the most 'left' of the top union officials is trapped by his social environment. Worse still, he has to work through an official machine whose personnel is very much a prisoner of this same environment.

The official is, and feels that he is, a member not of the working class but of the middle class. As one study based on interviews with hundreds of officials found:

> Most full-time officers rate themselves among the holders of middle-class posts (and rate their General Secretaries close to the top of a scale of social standing) . . . .
>
> (H. A. Clegg, A. J. Killick and Rex Adams, *Trade Union Officers*, Oxford, 1961, p. 90)

It is now normal for top trade union leaders to receive knighthoods or other state recognition — there are more knights or aspirant knights now than there were round King Arthur's table. It is normal for the top officials to get salaries well beyond their members' most fevered imaginings:

Take the case of the N U M. Immediately after the last national strike, the Executive met and endorsed wage rises of up to £2,100 a year, £40 a week, for national and area officials and area agents backdated to 1 January. This gives the union's national officials £7,100 a year.

In N A L G O the General Secretary's salary starts at

Socialist Worker, 1 September 1973

TRADE UNION OFFICIAL TRYING TO
AVOID A STRIKE

Carworker, September 1973

£10,000 and goes up to £11,000; the Deputy General
Secretary from £7,500 to £8,250; the two Assistant General
Secretaries from £6,600 to £7,333. At the same time
half the members of N A L G O earn less than £1,500;
typist-telephonists start at £807.

The General Secretary of the C P S A gets a salary of
£9,000 plus £7 a day subsistence allowance. The National
Negotiations Officer gets £5,000. An average clerical
worker member of C P S A earns £1,800.

The bureaucracy vs democracy

In some unions, even the formal trappings of democracy are
missing. In the E E P T U, for example, all full-time officials
are appointed by the Executive Council. The composition
of the Final Appeals Committee, for a long time made up
of 16 rank and file members, was changed in 1969. The
Rules then adopted state:

> The Executive Council shall appoint five of its members to constitute the Disciplinary Committee. The General President and General Secretary shall not be members of the Disciplinary Committee . . . The remaining members of the Executive Council shall constitute the Appeals Committee.

The Executive appointed itself judge, jury and prosecutor; and then, in 1971, to make the record look cleaner it changed the rule again; the Final Appeals Committee was to consist of three people selected by the General Secretary of the T U C.

The rule allowing for the election of rank and file trustees was also changed. Instead:

> The property and funds of the union shall rest in a sole corporate trustee . . . Such trustee shall be appointed by the Executive Council.

The set-up in the Iron and Steel Trades Confederation is hardly better. It is quite a common occurrence for the Executive to suspend and even expel local branch officers. On 8 July 1969 14 branch officials and official work representatives at the Corby steel works were suspended for leading an unofficial strike.

In the T & G W U, whose General Secretary is the Vice-President of the Institute of Workers' Control, the General Secretary is elected for life. At the last Rules Revision Conference, there were 12 resolutions on the agenda calling for the election of officers. They were defeated after a long and vehement speech by Jack Jones. A delegate to this Conference wrote to me:

> Jack Jones argued that you cannot get efficiency without job security. He argued that if a full-time officer did not get re-elected, he would have great difficulty in getting another job. A Scottish Road Haulage delegate rightly said that shop stewards have no security, so why should full-time officers expect it.
>
> Jack Jones again referred to the A U E W for his main argument. He said elections caused divisions and splits between right and left-wing groupings. He said this was the cause of troubles and difficulties in the A U E W. He emphasized that 'unity' must be kept.

123

The General Secretary is in a very strong position indeed. All national officers are directly accountable to him. A complicated Rule Book makes it easy for him to act practically at will.

The same delegate to the Rules Revision Conference added to his letter:

> The lay Executive meets only in order to listen to lengthy reports from Regions and Trade Groups. Although they meet for an entire week they basically can only rubber-stamp these reports. The reports only refer to past activities. The Executive very rarely gets the chance to shape future policy on specific issues. The Finance and General Purposes Committee – that is a sub-committee of the Executive – works in conjunction with the National Officials, and it is usually the case that the General Secretary runs the show. Consequently every General Secretary who is elected can build his own machine.

Even where democracy does prevail in theory, union leaders find a way round it. Take the case of the N U T.

On paper this union is very democratic. Its supreme body is the Annual Conference which should control its democratically elected Executive. 'As in other large unions, Conference is the ultimate source of authority, the chief instrument of democratic control, and the one great opportunity for rank and file members to review the Executive's work, and participate in the making of policy' (Dr W. Roy, *The Teachers' Union*, p. 92).

That at least is the theory. But as the Rank and File pamphlet, *Teachers' Salaries: The Fight for a Single Scale*, states:

> the Annual Conference is not truly representative of the membership at all – in terms of either the composition or the structure of delegacies. Since most voting at Conference is done by a show of hands rather than a card vote (where delegates vote with the full strength of their membership numbers) it is clear that the number of delegates an Association is entitled to is of crucial importance in policy making . . .
>
> . . . at the 1972 Conference, there was a delegate from the tiny Association of Llansilm, which could proudly boast a total

membership of *seven* (sic!). His vote was worth *well over one hundred times* that of his colleague from Birmingham who represented 404 members.

Then the workings of the Conference do everything to deflate the power of the rank and file:

It is important to look too at the actual procedure of Conference, to see what becomes of the resolutions from the rank and file, that were so carefully framed, discussed and amended in the Local Associations by the members themselves.

In 1974 over 100 resolutions on a wide variety of subjects were submitted by the local branches. Only six out of those 100 even managed to get a hearing at Conference. A bad year. But not especially so. There is a pattern over the years. In a speech to Conference in 1958 a delegate made the following observation: '. . . for each of the last four or five years, with the exception of this year, the number of motions submitted by Associations has been over 300 and the number of resolutions actually passed . . . as follows: 1954, 2; 1955, 9; 1956, 13; 1957, 15 . . . '

And what about the Executive of the N U T? What is its composition? The most significant feature of the N U T Executive is its domination by the Headteachers. In 1960 less than a quarter of the Executive were class teachers. In 1974 well over half the Executive are still Heads. So there is a situation where the hierarchical structure in the schools acts as a model for the structure of the union.

The Rank and File pamphlet quoted above comments:

. . . within the school the Head is the one person totally and arbitrarily responsible for the internal running of the establishment. The Local Education Authority vests in him or her the authority to do this and the Head is ultimately responsible not to his or her teachers, pupils or parents, but to the local authority who pays his or her salary. Is it really possible to expect someone who has this sort of relationship with the employer to perform, at the same time, the completely contradictory role of negotiator on behalf of the union? And yet this is exactly the situation.

In the period of the 'social contract', with the trade union leaders, employers and the government doing their utmost together to hold back wage demands, the question of union democracy, of who should own the union, its 11 million members or its full-time staff, will become more and more crucial. The question can be posed simply: 'will the unions make official all strikes in which workers defend their wages and conditions or will they not?' There is no doubt about the answer the trade union bureaucracy will give.

Fear of the masses; attachment to the status quo

One thing that terrifies the trade union bureaucrats more than anything else is the independent action of workers. Nothing is better calculated to cut down their importance, their status, their prestige. And nothing is more likely to strengthen their attachment to the status quo.

That attachment is not straightforward. The trade union bureaucrat is not a capitalist, but he's not a worker either. He lives off class struggle, but he can't let it go beyond the point of mediation, or negotiation. His basic rule is to keep the contestants alive and able to fight — gently.

The story goes — one cannot know how true it is — of a trade union leader speaking to a mass workers' meeting. He asked them: 'Do you want more money?' And to his

---

The trade union leader's dilemma

Are we sitting at the sickbed of capitalism, not only as doctors who want to cure the patient, but as prospective heirs who cannot wait for the end and would like to hasten it by administering poison? We are condemned, I think, to be doctors who seriously wish a cure, and yet we have to retain the feeling that we are heirs who wish to receive the entire legacy of the capitalist system today rather than tomorrow. This double role, doctor and heir, is a damned difficult task.

(Fritz Tarnow, at the German Social Democratic Party congress, 1931)

---

surprise the shout came back loud and clear: 'No'. 'Do you want more holidays?' Again the answer came: 'No!' Baffled, he asked, 'What do you want?' The reply was, 'We want the revolution'. He retorted: 'But that's not on. Management will never agree to that.'

There is a socialist, revolutionary logic, and a capitalist, reformist logic. The first argues: if the country is in great economic crisis, it is not the fault of the workers. It is not the workers of Britain who exchanged millions of pounds into marks, yen, francs, or dollars. It is not the workers who exported capital by the thousands of millions. It is not they who speculated in the commodity market or bought office blocks only to keep them empty. Why should workers pay the cost of the capitalist crisis?

The capitalist, reformist argument is the exact opposite: if the demands of the workers run counter to the requirements and needs of capitalism, then, for heaven's sake, in the name of gradualism, let's put capitalism on its feet first before we do anything about our own programme of promises. The reformist, gradualist argument might lead to 'jam tomorrow'; it leads to wage restraint today.

At the altar of the state

In 1915 the N U R, the Miners' Federation (now N U M) and the Transport Workers' Federation (now T & G W U) formed a Triple Alliance to come to each other's aid if any one of them were attacked or threatened. At the beginning of 1921 the mine owners gave notice of drastic wage cuts which were to operate from the end of March. The Miners' Federation rejected the terms, and a lockout began on 31 March. Declaring a state of emergency, the government moved troops into the coalfields and mounted machine guns at the pit heads. The other members of the Triple Alliance promised to withdraw their labour on 15 April. The long-delayed trial of strength between the unions and the government seemed at last to have come.

Nothing happened. On the eve of the strike the whole thing collapsed. The union leaders had no stomach for a fight.

In fact they had given in two years before. Nye Bevan tells vividly how Robert Smillie described to him an interview the leaders of the Triple Alliance had had in 1919 with David Lloyd George, the Prime Minister:

Lloyd George sent for the labour leaders, and they went, so Robert told me, 'truculently determined they would not be talked over by the seductive and eloquent Welshman'. At this Bob's eyes twinkled in his grave, strong face. 'He was quite frank with us from the outset,' Bob went on. 'He said to us:

"Gentlemen, you have fashioned, in the Triple Alliance of the unions represented by you, a most powerful instrument. I feel bound to tell you that in our opinion we are at your mercy. The army is disaffected and cannot be relied upon. Trouble has occurred already in a number of camps. We have just emerged from a great war and the people are eager for the reward of their sacrifices, and we are in no position to satisfy them. In these circumstances, if you carry out your threat and strike, then you will defeat us."

How the trade union leaders fought the General Strike in 1926

Ben Tillett (TGWU):

'We want peace in our time, O Lord, we do.'

Jimmy Thomas (NUR):

'We have striven, we have pleaded, we have begged for peace, because we want peace. We still want peace. The nation wants peace. Those who want war must take the responsibility.'

'I know the Government's position. I have never disguised that in a challenge to the Constitution, God help us unless the Government won . . . but this is not only not a revolution, it is not something that says, "We want to overthrow everything".'

'What I dreaded about this strike more than anything else was this . . . If by any chance it should have got out of the hands of those who would be able to exercise some control, every sane man knows what would have happened . . . That danger, that fear, was always in our mind.'

Charles Dukes (GMWU):

'Every day the strike proceeded the control and the authority of the dispute was passing out of the hands of responsible executives into the hands of men who had no authority, no control, and was wrecking the movement from one end to the other.'

J.R. Clynes (TGWU):

'I do not fear, on this subject, to throw such weight as I have on the side of caution. I am not in fear of the capitalist class. The only class I fear is our own.'

"But if you do so," went on Mr Lloyd George, "have you weighed the consequences? The strike will be in defiance of the government of the country and by its very success will precipitate a constitutional crisis of the first importance. For, if a force arises in the state which is stronger than the state itself, then it must be ready to take on the functions of the state, or withdraw and accept the authority of the state. Gentlemen," asked the Prime Minister quietly, "have you considered, and if you have, are you ready?" 'From that moment on,' said Robert Smillie, 'we were beaten and we knew we were.'

(Aneurin Bevan, *In Place of Fear,* London, 1952 pp. 20-21)

If Lloyd George told a *revolutionary* workers' leader 'I feel bound to tell you that in our opinion we are at your mercy. The army is disaffected and cannot be relied upon', the revolutionary would have answered, 'Excellent! Move over. We are taking power!'

But trade union bureaucrats would never dare to violate the 'National Constitution', or to question the neutrality of the state, for these are their sacred cows, and the most important source of their ideological paralysis.

In conclusion

All the national union leaders take it for granted that they operate within the system, and intuitively accept that they can only operate successfully if the system itself enjoys success. They hope against hope that capitalism will continue to prosper, as in the past, so that their own form of trade unionism can continue to prosper with it. All national trade union leaders, whether 'left' or right, accept the separation between industrial and political struggle. They view the industrial struggle of workers inside the existing society as something quite distinct from any political action to transform this society.

As the crisis of capitalism deepens this stance will become a greater and greater hindrance to the mobilization of workers in defence of their living standards and their jobs, a defence that can no longer be separated from readiness to challenge capitalism as a system of society.

130

8.
The Need to Build a Rank and File Movement

There is a clear discrepancy between the state of morale and the organizational readiness for battle in both the capitalist camp and the working-class camp. The ruling class is suffering from a loss of nerve but has a relatively strong, centralized organization inherited from the past. Amongst workers the position is precisely the opposite: the state of morale and confidence is excellent, but the level of organization, its structure and staffing, are really appalling. That too is an inheritance from the past.

Such discrepancies cannot go on for ever. Either morale gives way and adapts itself to the slate of organization, or organization adapts to the state of morale. Which it is to be depends very much on the ability of socialists and militants to build a rank and file movement of trade unionists.

Co-existence of rank and file militants and trade union bureaucracy

For a quarter of a century after the Second World War the trade union bureaucracy did little damage to rank and file organization, even though it nearly always opposed workers' strikes and collaborated fully with the employers and the state. In some cases the bureaucracy did smash the rank and file — for instance at British Light Steel Pressings (1961) or at Ford, Dagenham (1962). But usually management retreated under the duress of the short-lived strikes that were typical of the period before the trade union bureaucracy managed to intervene effectively and discipline the workers. Capitalism was quite prosperous in those years and the employers were ready to give way without prolonged and widespread battles. Strikes were on the whole unofficial, short-lived and small.

In 1936, according to the Ministry of Labour, about one third of strikes were official (H. A. Turner, *The Trend of Strikes,* Leeds, 1963, p. 14). Thirty years later the proportion had dropped to about one twentieth. And if account were taken of the strikes which do not get recorded, the proportion would be even smaller. Minute sums were spent on strike benefits – a total for all unions of only £462,000 or about 11d per union member per year in 1963 (Royal Commission on Trade Unions and Employers' Associations, *Written Evidence of the Ministry of Labour,* London, p. 52). Death benefits were larger at £1,011,000. Clearly union members got more from their organizations when dead and buried than when they were alive and fighting.

The overwhelming majority of strikes were very short – 3.3 days per worker on strike in 1953-64 compared with 32.2 in 1919-26, or 10.6 in 1927-38. They were normally so short that it did not matter much whether union headquarters supported them or not. In many cases a central element in militants' tactics was to win *before* trade union headquarters heard about it!

The strategy, if one may grace the chaotic, spontaneous, tactically blind reaction of the industrial rank and file militants over two decades with this word, was simple: let the national leadership of the trade unions deal with industry-wide bargaining, fixing the floor of wages, and let the shop stewards deal with local bargaining to raise the ceiling. What the militant cared most about was the latter, wage drift. Bargaining within the individual firm took place over such matters as piecework and other forms of payment by results, additions to wage rates such as bonuses and local rules and practices including the manning of machines and demarcation questions.

Democracy on the shop floor managed to co-exist with bureaucracy in the trade union structure ... The shop stewards' committees always relied on the union machine in lesser issues against management (court cases about accidents and so on) and they often found it important to get official recognition for strike action in order to get the support of the more backward members in their own place of work.

(T. Cliff, 'On Perspectives', *International Socialism*, no 36, April-May 1969)

Changes over the last few years

A radical change in the pattern of strikes has taken place over the last few years. There are many more large-scale and prolonged strikes:

	Number of workers involved (thousands)	Number of working days lost (thousands)	Average number of days per worker on strike
1953-64 (average)	1,081	3,712	3.3
1965	876	2,925	3.3
1966	544	2,398	4.4
1967	734	2,787	4.0
1968	2,258	4,680	2.1
1969	1,665	6,876	4.1
1970	1,801	10,980	6.1
1971	1,171	13,551	12.1
1972	1,734	23,909	13.8

In 1972 the total of 23,909,000 working days lost through stoppages was 3½ times higher than in 1969 and five times higher than the yearly average for the previous 19 years. The total exceeded that of any other year in the 20 years.

These figures do not include *political* strikes. In 1971, the Department of Employment and Productivity estimated that nearly four million days were lost through political strikes. The same exclusion applied in 1972.

The figures [for 1972 – T C] exclude absences from work between 24 July and 26 July by about 170,000 workers in various parts of the country, including 40,000 dock workers, in protest against the decision to commit five London dockworkers to prison for contempt of the National Industrial Relations Court; absences on 18 December by about 55,000 engineering workers, mainly in London and the south-east, Oxford and Sheffield, demonstrating against the fine imposed on the Amalgamated Union of Engineering Workers by the National Industrial Relations Court; and on 20 December by about 160,000 engineering workers, supported by 10,000 dockworkers, mainly in the West Midlands and on Merseyside, and also in Manchester, Hull, Dundee and Bristol, demonstrating for the same reason.

(*Department of Employment and Productivity Gazette,* June 1973, p. 554)

The statistics probably also exclude several strikes in support of pensions during November, notably at the British Steel Corporation's Anchor site.

Under these conditions of sharpening class struggle, even the most right-wing trade union bureaucracies have given ground to rank and file pressure. Take the case of the G M W U. It completely opposed the strike of 11,000 Pilkington workers from 3 April to 21 May 1970. It then opposed the 48-day strike of 5,000 G K N workers. Shortly afterwards it opposed a three-week strike by 3,000 gas workers in the Midlands. But fear of losing complete control over his rank and file, or fear of their leaving the G M W U to join other unions, forced Lord Cooper, General Secretary at the time, to give support to a number of other strikes. The change can be seen from the amount the G M W U spent on strike pay: 1967 £17,700; 1968 £84,000; 1969 £107,000; 1970 £713,000. In the last year of the series the G M W U was spending more in strike pay than the whole trade union movement in 1963!

In their day Deakin and Carron opposed practically *all* strikes; today Basset and Chapple, not to say Jones and Scanlon, support many (or at least they did prior to the 'social contract'). This does not mean that the bureaucracy has become less of a dead weight on workers' struggles than it was during the 25 years after the Second World War. On the contrary, when management was relatively soft and strikes short, opposition from the trade union bureaucracy hardly affected the workers' ability to win one way or the

134

other. Today, with the bureaucracy actively involved in disputes, its readiness to compromise with management and its attempts to dampen workers' initiative are more effectively a burden on workers' struggles.

This explains why, side by side with the victory of the miners in 1972, we had the defeat of the engineers in their national wage claim; and why the same story was again repeated in 1974. It explains how some sections of the trade union movement won important victories in recent years while others, like the gas workers, hospital ancillary workers, civil servants, and teachers, lost in 1973.

The record, 1973

1973 was a very bad year.

When the miners decided not to go on strike, and accepted the £1 plus 4 per cent norm of Phase Two, they were followed by the dockers and other, weaker sections of the working class – gas workers who accepted the government norm after a work to rule, an overtime ban and selective strikes, civil servants, teachers and nurses.

The engineers were completely chained to the government's norms: up to the end of November wage settlements in engineering averaged 7 per cent (*Engineering Employers' Federation News,* February 1974). The strike movement in engineering declined sharply during the year:

Industrial disputes in engineering 1972 and 1973

	No. of strikes	Average days lost per strike	Total days lost
1972	1,054	3,543	4,190,894
1973	1,235	1,511	1,865,748

Official strikes almost disappeared; there were eleven involving manual workers with an average of 5,508 and a total of 60,585 days lost, compared with 39 in 1972 with an average of 24,902 and a total of 971,172 days lost. For staff workers the 1973 figures show 22 strikes, each averaging 954 and totalling 20,995 days lost, compared with ten in 1972, each averaging 8,697 and totalling 86,974 days lost.

Overall class struggle took a dip in 1973. Whereas in 1972 there were 1,734 stoppages involving 1,734,000 workers with 23,909,000 days lost, in 1973 there were 2,902 stoppages involving 1,513,000 workers, with 7,197,000 days of strike. The average strike in 1972 went on for 13.8 days, in 1973 for only 4.8 days. On the whole workers did not win the battles of 1973. Not only did the gas workers, civil servants and hospital workers lose, but also many of the workers who participated in the numerous small, fragmented strikes that took place. As a result, wage drift practically disappeared: in the first quarter it was 8.5 per cent; in the second quarter it was negative – minus 0.5 per cent; in the third quarter it was again negative – minus 0.4 per cent; only in the last quarter did drift reappear with some strength, 1.3 per cent (*National Institute Economic Review,* May 1974, p. 17).

1974 – A general rise in the struggle

The year started with a magnificent victory to the miners not only on the wages front, but also on the political. The Tories were forced to the country and lost office.

The first sections of the working class to confront the newly elected Labour government were the local government workers, teachers and nurses. At practically the same time, in April, the leadership of the Confederation of Engineering Workers signed a national agreement that gave mere peanuts to the two million workers involved – only 2 to 2½ per cent, or one third of the 7 per cent allowed under Phase Three.

The capitulation of the engineers' leaders delayed but did not stop the action of the rank and file. A few months later numerous strikes broke out in engineering, including the most advanced, best organized, traditionally most militant section — the car workers.

There has never been as much variety and unevenness in struggle as now. Tiny fragments of strikes still take place; but next to them there are massive ones. Small strikes sometimes lead to very large ones: at the time of writing, small groups of lorry drivers in Scotland are spreading their action into a strike of huge proportions. There are fantastic combinations of the most advanced methods of workers' struggle — factory occupations, flying pickets — with the most modest claims. Here and there a group of workers who have not much tradition of trade unionism move far ahead and then retreat; while more experienced sections are sometimes slow to move. The variety, the flux, is very exciting and defies a dogmatic, rigid approach.

Some quite large strikes have taken place in recent months: for wage parity — Perkins, Hawker Siddeley, Chrysler, Auto-Machinery; for staff status — Vauxhall, the millwrights in Chrysler Coventry; for restoring the skill differentials eroded during Phases One, Two and Three — Swan-Hunter Tyneside, Sunderland Shipbuilders, Burroughs Cumbernauld. There have been strikes for ending Friday night shifts — Ford Halewood; Goodyear Glasgow; and over shop stewards' rights and against victimization of militants — Cowley Stoke, Briant's Birmingham, Birmid Qualcast Birmingham.

Factory occupations have mushroomed, not only to resist closure, but also in the fight for higher wages, threshold payments, bonuses, etc. Here is a short list culled from the industrial reports in *Socialist Worker:*

- Rushton Paxman diesel factory, Lancs: 100 workers, for reinstatement of John Deason, A U E W shop steward, 7 weeks.
- Charles McNeil engineering works, Kinning Park, Glasgow: for better wages.
- 200 A U E W members, mostly Pakistanis, at Punfield and Barstow (N W London): for better wages.

137

- 150 workers at Dresser Europe factory at Bracknell, Berks.: for a second threshold increase.
- 250 workers at Hick Hargreaves, Bolton: for better wages.
- 6,000 workers at Plessey Telecommunications in Beeston, Notts.: threshold payment.
  Workers at Coles Cranes, Sunderland: 12 weeks' strike, for pay.
- 400 women at Salford Electrical Instruments, Heywood, Lancs.: for equal bonus.
- 400 hospital workers at Hammersmith Hospital W London: for pay increase.

Over the last couple of years, there must have been at least 100 factory occupations.

Then look at the flying pickets. The miners and the building workers used them with dramatic effect in 1972. Now again they are spreading. The current strike by 6,000 lorry drivers in Scotland has spread thanks to the flying pickets from the Greenock Container Terminal. There has been picketing in Edinburgh and Leith. Road haulage depots and docks have had lorries turned away by picket lines of up to 70 (*Socialist Worker*, 26 October 1974).

There has probably never been a period like the present in Britain for the sheer variety of working-class struggles.

Black workers enter the scene

One of the most exciting features of the present time is the rise of black workers to industrial militancy. Black workers They live in the worst housing, overcrowded, insanitary, and pay the highest rents for it. On top of the oppression of boss and landlord, the police harass blacks — demanding passports, planting drugs, inventing charges, allowing or encouraging others to attack black people. And if they fight back, black workers find union officials even more indifferent to their needs than white workers do. Unfortunately, white workers are often completely indifferent to their

138

black fellows.

Here is a report drawn up by a black comrade on three strikes by black workers in London over the last year or so:

S T C, July-August 1973

300 workers, mainly A U E W, walked out over the refusal of E T U members to train a West Indian as a setter. Only four white members including the convenor struck. All the white A U E W stewards crossed the picket line. The A U E W District Committee took no action against the stewards, and failed to call on other A U E W members not to cross the picket line. Officials visited the factory but made no call for A U E W members not to cross the picket line. No collections were organized. Calls were made for Scanlon and Birch to intervene but nothing happened.

Perivale-Gutterman, March 1974

60 Pakistani and Indian workers were provoked into strike action by management who had stocked up with raw materials. Scabs were recruited and smashed through the picket line. No attempt was made by the T & G W U to organize more pickets. After eight weeks the strikers were demoralized. The T & G W U told them to apply to the Industrial Tribunal for compensation for unfair dismissal. Very few got compensation; all lost their jobs. The trade union organization which the Pakistanis had built was smashed.

This factory was in the biggest industrial area in Ealing, but the T & G W U made no attempt to organize help from other T & G W U members at all.

Punfield and Barstow, May-June 1974

120 A U E W members, mainly Pakistani workers, oc-cupied the factory over loss of wages due to the three-day week. After three days they left the factory for the weekend. They were locked out on Monday morning. There was no money from the union for six

weeks, nor any social security payments received, and the union did not help to get it.

The District Committee did not organize pickets or financial support. Local International Socialists took strikers around local factories, and even suggested tactics. They re-occupied the factory once, but the promised support from the District Committee did not arrive. The attempt collapsed after half a day due to police harassment.

After eight weeks the union officials accepted the management position that the factory was closed down. All the strikers lost their jobs, and officials advised strikers to apply to the Industrial Tribunal for unfair dismissal. Few got any compensation.

The most famous case is the strike of 500 Asian workers at Imperial Typewriters, Leicester. This is the story as told in *Socialist Worker:*

'When I joined the factory', said one woman striker, 'I never knew what a union was, nor a shop steward. Now we want to select our own shop stewards. We have so many grievances and the foreman never listens.' Low wages, racial discrimination and continual cheating over a bonus scheme proved too much for 500 Asian workers at the factory and in a spontaneous outburst of rage they determined to organize themselves against their ruthless penny-pinching management.

Forty strikers, led by 27 women, came out demanding £500 they had been swindled out of under a bonus scheme. They were soon followed by hundreds of other Asians who struck with a host of complaints against both management and the union.

Until then all shop stewards had been white and normally appointed by Reg Weaver, who has been Transport Workers' Union convenor for 22 years. He supports the management sacking 270 of the strikers and has even threatened a strike by some of the white workers if the strike leaders are allowed to return to work.

George Bromley, T & G W U District Secretary is a long-standing trade unionist. He too vehemently attacks the strike and supports the settlement. In racist Leicester it is not easy for Asians to get strikes made official. So the strikers bypassed the local union leaders and took a fleet of buses to Transport House in London. Jack Jones was embarrassed at the publicity and offered an internal union inquiry – but said nothing about making the strike official.

Still the 500 stayed out, determined but unpaid by the union and unable to get social security. They are demanding a new wages system where they are not cheated over the bonus and underpaid, equal opportunities with white workers and no discrimination. They are determined that there will be no victimization.

('Black Workers Betrayed Again . . . and Again . . . ', *Socialist Worker*, 20 July 1974)

There have been many many more strikes by black workers over the last couple of years. To mention a few: Injection Mouldings, Mansfield Hosiery, Nuneaton Art Castings, Colmore Depot (B M C Birmingham), Bradford Bakery (Birmingham), the Slough Combined Optical Industries, where the Asian workers won a magnificent victory recently. It is not easy for black workers. They suffer from

● having to work very often in sweat shops and in badly organized workplaces;
● having to take the worst jobs in the factories where traditions of struggle are minimal;
● indifference if not hostility from trade union officials, and racialist attitudes among many white workers.

But notwithstanding all the difficulties, black workers are on the move, are full of fighting spirit and are clearly ready to make heavy sacrifices for the things they believe in.

Women workers enter the scene

There is no statistical account of the strikes in which women are involved, nor is it known how many women workers participate in them. But there is no doubt at all

141

that both have risen very significantly in recent months.*

These strikes have been of many shapes and sizes. Some were very long, far longer than most men's strikes, as can be seen from the following few examples:

Salford Electrical Instruments, Eccles — 11 weeks

GEC Spon Street, Coventry — 8 weeks' dispute

Slumberland Beds, Paisley — (mainly women) 19 weeks, with factory occupation lasting 15 weeks

Imperial Typewriters, Leicester — (mainly women) 3 months

Wingrove & Rogers, Liverpool — 17 weeks

Salford Electrical Instruments, Heywood — 10 weeks

Blackpool Empire Pools — over 4 months

In a relatively large number of cases the strike started in protest at victimization of shop stewards or convenors. Examples are:

Coops, Wigan — strike over the sacking of a shop steward.

Plessey, London — strike over the sacking of senior shop steward Kath Kelly who had worked at the plant for 23 years.

Easterbrook & Allcard Presto, Sheffield — a strike over the sacking of the convenor Sylvia Greenwood.

Wilderpool Sports Centre, Warrington — strike over the sacking of shop steward Maureen Spiers.

Armstrong Patents, Beverley — strike over the sacking of the convenor Jean Jepson.

Very many of the strikes end in defeat — a far greater proportion than men's strikes.

In many areas the strike is reported as being the first in the factory after many many years of 'normalcy' ('peace'), sometimes as many as 20 years as in the Osram, G E C

---

* A list of strikes collated from reports in *Socialist Worker* and the *Morning Star* was made by Sheila Rowbotham (*Red Rag*, no 5), and Dave Phillips and Margaret Edney (*Red Rag*, no 8). I found both extremely useful and have borrowed from them extensively.

factory in Erith. In practically all cases they were one-off affairs, sparked off by groups of workers, new to the factory, with very little industrial, not to speak of trade union, experience, as in Kenilworth Components, Leicester, or the Wyuna Corset factory in Southall.

Decisive to the fate of the strikes have been the attitudes of other workers to the women. The Wingrove and Rogers' strikers won because no lorries crossed the picket line, because the dockers and railwaymen blacked supplies to the factory and finally because the District Committee of the A U E W threatened a one-day strike in the whole of Merseyside. Under that threat the management caved in.

Again the workers on strike in Maclaren Controls (I T T) won after 300 shop stewards in the Glasgow area gave a pledge to step up support and blacking, and after steps were taken to set up an I T T Combine committee of shop stewards.

Unfortunately, in the majority of cases the women workers got no support and were beaten.

Since women workers are almost invariably in a weaker position than men, outside support is more crucial to them. Even arranging simple activities like picketing or the send-

WOMEN ONLY WORK SO THEY CAN BUY LUXURIES...

Women's Voice, No 9 January 1974

ing of delegations imposes a heavy burden on women, far heavier than on men workers. Who will look after the children? How are they to counter tactics such as those used by the management of Salford Electrical Instruments, Heywood, who persuaded the local authorities to shut the nurseries to children of women on strike since they now had the time to look after them themselves?

To take even the simplest step, women workers need to *generalize* their struggle: to get the support of other workers and of housewives in the neighbourhood.

They need to organize delegations to other factories in the same towns and other towns to collect money. They have to appeal to the Executive Committees of the relevant trade unions through as many union bodies as they can to make the strike official. They have to call on all the relevant unions to expel members who scab. One can be lenient sometimes with a man who scabs on men; but there can be no tolerating men who scab on women, as women are in a much weaker position.

Women workers need to generalize the struggle for another reason also. They are in the lowest-paid jobs. As we have seen, nearly nine-tenths of women manual workers earn a basic wage of under £25 a week. They need, at the very least, the £30 minimum, made proof against inflation. But this fight for higher wages will not get far unless it becomes part of a wider movement to eliminate low grades of pay as such. The best example to follow is the three weeks' strike by S O G A T against the British Printing Industries Federation and the Newspaper Society in 1974. The *Financial Times, Mirror* and *The Times* were stopped. Faced with the threat that other papers might be involved, the employers caved in. The result: Grade 4 has been abolished in the print; 50,000 women have moved from Grade 4 to Grade 3; all the women transferred got 95 per cent of the Grade 3 rate in October 1974; by March 1975 they will be on 97½ per cent of the rate; and in October

1975 — 100 per cent.

Part of escaping from low-paid jobs is through forcing entry for women into skilled occupations. In 1973 there were 26,880 boy apprentices in manufacturing and only *452* girls. Altogether the number of apprentices in the country (1972) was:

Boys — 473,000 (or 42 per cent of all boys employed).

Girls — 9,000 (or 7 per cent of all girls employed).

Of the girl apprentices over three-quarters were in hairdressing.

While 39.7 per cent of boys went to day release classes, only 10.42 per cent of the girls did.

Day release should be made compulsory. Apprenticeships should be opened to girls. It is pure prejudice to believe that women are less able to be skilled engineers than men. As a matter of fact it takes more physical exertion to be a machine-minder as many women are, than to be a machine-setter, which women are not.

In a period of inflation we cannot afford these petty prejudices. The number of women at work is about three-quarters the number of men; 80 per cent of them work full-time; 50 per cent are married. Their wage has become a *normal* constituent of the family income. More and more women are being forced into the struggle; the men ignore their vast, untapped reserves of militancy at their peril.

Women are half the adult working class. In their own interests, in the interests of their children and families, and in the interests of the whole working class they need to join the wider struggle. Room will have to be found for them in that wider struggle.

Inflation — pressure for unity of the working class

Inflation hurts all workers equally and must lead to greater and greater similarity of response. It also increases the need for the unity of all workers in struggle. Jimmy McCallum (T A S S, John Brown Engineering, Clydebank) put it extremely well in an article about the strikes taking place in Scotland. All these strikes he wrote,

> have one thing in common. Not one is official. A parade of senior trade union officials, particularly from the Transport Workers' Union, have come to Scotland to tell their members about the virtues of the 'social contract' and to instruct them to get back to work ...
>
> Fortunately, the workers in Scotland know more than their union leaders about the way inflation is eating into their wage packets. They have little faith in the 'social contract' and are taking their action now before the freeze. They are rejecting their officials' advice because they know from bitter experience what the Labour government's promises can mean.
>
> The problem is this: because the strike movement is unofficial, each group of workers sees itself as fighting its own battle. The lorry drivers think they will win on their own. The Corporation bus workers have not linked their fight to other local authority strikes such as the sewage workers, the dustbin men and the teachers.
>
> Only the weakest sections on strike see the need for concerted action, because they need it most.
>
> This fragmentation in the strike movement must be overcome. Links must be built between each dispute.
>
> The fragmentation of these disputes and the hostility of the trade union leadership towards this strike movement underlines the need for rank and file organization. If a powerful rank and file organization of trade unionists existed, each of the disputes could have been connected together, and given solidarity and assistance.
>
> The opportunities for building a rank and file organization have never been better.
>
> (*Socialist Worker,* 26 October 1974)

In building such an organization it is important to learn from the movements of the past, both their successes and their failures.

The first shop stewards' movement

An unprecedented wave of working-class struggles started in 1910. Britain was engulfed by larger and larger unofficial strikes, starting with the miners in Northumberland and Durham and culminating in a strike of immense revolutionary significance, the Dublin Transport Workers' strike. Railway workers, miners, engineers, seamen, dockers, cotton workers – the entire labour movement was drawn into the struggle.

The war did not stop the rising wave of militancy. It continued until 1919. Never before or since has the British working class scaled such heights.

The struggles were on a massive scale – 200,000 miners came out in South Wales in April 1915, 200,000 engineers in 48 towns in May 1917. The readiness of workers to do battle and the level of their solidarity were amazing. One story is worth telling: in November 1916 a Sheffield engineer, Leonard Hargreaves, was conscripted into the army. His mates thought he was being victimized, so:

> The Shop Stewards' Committee of Sheffield demanded that he be released in line with government assurances, and a mass meeting held under its auspices on 13 November threatened to strike unless its demands were complied with. On the 15th, Hargreaves was released from the army, and the government agreed to meet the society to devise a scheme which would meet their objections. This news did not reach the Sheffield workers and on 16 November they struck work as planned, and two days later workers from Barrow-in-Furness came out in sympathy. Work was resumed only when Hargreaves appeared on the platform at a mass meeting of the men and confirmed that he had been released unconditionally.
>
> (J. B. Jefferys, *The Story of the Engineers*, London, 1946, pp. 181-82)

A mass strike in defence of one worker!

The strikes were all unofficial, directed not only against the employers, but also against the government and the trade union leaders. Their central theme was resistance to industrial compulsion. They and they alone maintained the de facto right to strike.

Out of those struggles emerged an organization of the rank and file: the National Movement of Shop Stewards and Workers' Committees, based primarily on Glasgow and Sheffield. The movement created a National Administrative Council in 1917.

Inevitably, the movement was led into a political confrontation with the government on the question of war or peace. It came to a head in January 1918 in response to the Russian revolutionaries' appeal for peace, and to the severe shortages and steeply rising prices of food at home.

The rank and file movement during the war was groping towards the idea of workers' power embodied in workers' councils – in soviets – and towards the rejection of the parliamentary road to socialism. As James Hinton writes:

> The enthusiasm with which sections of the left took up and developed the soviet idea in Britain is to be explained not only by understandable elation over the Russian revolution, but also, and primarily, by the fact that this idea answered to a real theoretical need felt by British revolutionaries as a result of their own domestic experience. . .
>
> The leaders of the shop stewards' movement had been quick to see a parallel between the workers' committees and the Russian soviets.
>
> (James Hinton, *The First Shop Stewards' Movement*, London: George Allen and Unwin, 1973, p. 307)

However, there were a number of weaknesses in the movement: It covered only engineering workers, and then only those in munitions production. Not even all munitions workers were involved.

> Apart from Glasgow and Sheffield there were three other centres in which munitions production . . . predominated. In none of these centres, Woolwich, Barrow or the Tyne, did the shop stewards' movement ever exist as a permanent and effective organization.   (Hinton, p. 178)

148

In the Midlands the picture was even more abysmal. In Birmingham efforts to establish a workers' committee failed, and the Coventry Workers' Committee was primarily a propaganda body.

The movement suffered from a craft-consciousness that made the inclusion of semi-skilled and unskilled workers, including women, practically impossible.

The movement was also very loose — very anti-centralist. This gave the government a tremendous advantage and ultimately led to a debacle in January 1918. In fighting the *trade union* leaders, the movement fell into principled opposition to *all leaders*.

Attitude to work in the trade union machine

A further weakness of the shop stewards' movement was its lack of a clear attitude towards work in the trade union machine. They distrusted the union bureaucracy and asserted the independence of the rank and file, but they did not go further and campaign directly for full-time union office. As the Clyde Workers' Committee put it in November 1915,

> We will support the officials just so long as they rightly represent the workers, but we will act independently immediately they misrepresent them. Being composed of delegates from every shop and untrammelled by obsolete rule or law, we claim to represent the true feeling of the workers. We can act immediately according to the merits of the case and the desire of the rank and file.
>
> (Quoted by Hinton, p. 296)

Part of the reason for their abstentionism in trade union matters was undoubtedly their poverty in personnel. They simply did not have the people to stand for union office. Nor, had they tried, would

> the revolutionary shop stewards . . . have made any very substantial inroads into trade union officialdom . . . In most areas the appeal of their distinctive policies was limited to a small

149

minority of the more militant workers.
(Hinton, p. 293)

Attitude to work in the trade union branches

The shop stewards were also undecided on their attitude to work in the branches. In some places, Sheffield for instance, they stressed the importance of such work. The Workers' Committee there,

> representing the great majority of local engineering workers, worked closely with the A S E District Committee, the two structures acting as 'legal' and 'illegal' wings of a single organization. One of the most prominent members of the Sheffield Committee, Ted Lismer, was also a local official of his union, the Steam Engine Makers.
> (Hinton, p. 293)

In other places they ignored the local union machine.

The importance of working at local level, within the unions can hardly be exaggerated. It was brought home quite recently at the Saltley Coke Depot mass picket, one of the most important rank and file actions in recent years, when 10,000 Birmingham engineers turned up to the miners' picket line and helped them to victory.

'We must be in the unions, of the unions, but not determined by their limitations.'
J.T. Murphy

The story begins on 1 February 1972 when the Birmingham *Evening Mail* carried a story on the Saltley Depot. It revealed the Depot as the only big stockpile of coal left in the country. In the previous fortnight stocks had been reduced from 130,000 tons to less than 100,000 tons. About 250 lorries a day from all over the country were loading up. On 4 February miners' pickets moved into the city. However, the 200 pickets who turned up got nowhere. Only 15 lorries refused to cross the picket line. Next day the picketing broke into scuffles, and two miners were arrested. On Monday, 7 February, 1,000 miners turned up to the picket line, but still lorries got through. That day four policemen and two pickets were taken to hospital; 13 pickets were arrested.

The Labour movement in Birmingham then started to move. S U Carburettors came out on 1 February. But more than that was needed. This is where the Birmingham East District Committee of the A U E W came to play a crucial role. On Tuesday, 8 February, Arthur Scargill addressed the District Committee. It decided unanimously to call for strike action and a mass picket on 10 February. The following afternoon the senior stewards in the District met and decided to bring out their factories and march to the Saltley gates for 10 a.m. the next day. Fifty thousand engineering workers came out, and more than 10,000 marched.

There are many large factories near Saltley, including Dunlop with more than 5,000 workers, Tractors and Transmissions with 4,500, Pressed Steel Fisher, Castle Bromwich, with 13,000, S U Carburettors with 1,500. That day, the 10th, other unions made it clear that their members also would be out if the gates of Saltley re-opened, and the A U E W District Committee stated that they would be out again if that happened.

10 February was a grand victory for the alliance of miners and engineering workers. The police were helpless, all lorries were stopped. It was the final shot in the final battle of the miners.

Weakness of politics in the first shop stewards' movement

The shop stewards' movement as such did not take a clear stand on the key political issue of the day — the war.

151

There were of course a few individuals who did take a very clear anti-war position, the most notable being John Maclean. But the movement as a whole fudged the issue.

One important reason for this political weakness was the smallness of the revolutionary socialist parties. They were minute. The most important revolutionary group in Glasgow, the Socialist Labour Party, had about 100 members in 1915. The British Socialist Party had less. In Sheffield, the other main centre of the shop stewards' movement, they were even smaller.

Another important reason lay in its leadership's tendency towards syndicalism, a militant view of capitalism which places heavy emphasis on social relations at the point of production to the neglect of almost everything else. It is particularly forgetful of the roles of the state and of the revolutionary party, and therefore blind to the interaction between workers' 'spontaneous' industrial activity and political action.

This lack of politics contributed substantially to the final collapse of the shop stewards' movement. An appeal, in January 1918, for a strike against the war ended in complete fiasco. The government stole the shop steward leaders' thunder by introducing food rationing, and the mass of engineering workers ignored the call. The leaders of the movement had not prepared them for it politically.

The Minority Movement

Three years after its founding conference, the Communist Party launched a new rank and file movement, the Minority Movement. The new movement overcame a number of the defects of the wartime shop stewards' movement. It organized widely, not only amongst engineers, but also amongst miners, building workers, railwaymen and other workers. It was not crippled by craft prejudice. It was not a loose movement, but a highly centralist organization.

It suffered nonetheless from a number of serious weaknesses. It was built when the rank and file was very much on the defensive. Coalmining, textiles, shipbuilding and engineering were all badly hit by the slump of 1921, and at no time since then had unemployment fallen much lower than 1½ million. On 15 April 1921, Black Friday, the miners were left fighting a battle which they lost with disastrous consequences three months later. On 4 July, a general cotton lockout took place. Then came the turn of the engineers, beaten after a 14-week lockout which began in March 1922. What remained of the wartime shop stewards' movement was smashed. The militants were left outside the gates of the factory and 'the shop stewards' committees [were reduced] to propaganda bodies within the unions' (Murphy, p. 208). The result was inevitable:

The Minority Movement remained . . . primarily an organization for propaganda in the branches, rather than an organization for action in the workshops.

(Hinton, p. 329)

The Movement was not helped by the policy of reliance on the T U C 'left' imposed on the Communist Party by the Stalinist leadership of the Communist International.

The Communist Party's factory base was very weak at that time. As late as May 1925, 'there were only 68 Communist factory groups, embracing a mere 10 per cent of the party membership' (Brian Pearce, *Some Rank and File Movements,* a Labour Review pamphlet, London, 1959, p. 19).

The way ahead

We can learn a number of things from the rank and file movement of 1910-18:

First, to distrust completely the trade union bureaucracy — whether right or 'left'.

Second, to place complete confidence in the ability and the potentialities of the rank and file, confidence in the

power of the workers which reveals itself most strongly in periods of mass struggles.

Third, to prize above everything the development of the class consciousness of working people.

Fourth, to believe that in the struggle, while workers are trying to defend themselves, they change themselves, and become capable of creating a new society.

We have a number of advantages over the shop stewards' movement of half a century ago.

The workers today are much more confident and demanding than they were then. The bosses and the trade union bureaucrats call them 'bloody-minded', but this is all to the good.

OH NO — THEY'RE ALL PULLING TOGETHER !

Socialist Worker, 3 March 1973

Second, shop organization is much stronger at present than it has ever been. Today we have 300,000 shop stewards!

Third, our shop stewards' organization is not only larger in size, but also much more evenly spread among industries and regions. A shop stewards' movement would engulf much more than the handful of areas it embraced then.

Fourth, in the First World War great combines were largely limited to the munitions industries, and for this reason the shop stewards' movement was largely limited to the main munitions centres — Clydeside and Sheffield; to-day giant firms with plants in all parts of the country, and even abroad, predominate in *every* field of industry. A shop stewards' movement today could be much more universal.

Fifth, craft attitudes are far less prevalent now and are bound to do much less damage than half a century ago.

As against this, we face a number of disadvantages in building an effective national rank and file movement.

First, the movement then reflected the great victory of the October revolution — this was decisive in terms of its morale. We have no backing like this.

Second, the shop stewards' movement was led by people who had earned national prominence in mass strikes, Tom Mann, J. T. Murphy, A. J. Cook, Willie Gallacher, Arthur MacManus, and others. Because the industrial struggle over the last generation has been fragmented, there are no leaders of similar national prominence at present.

Finally, the struggle today is not an all-or-nothing battle as it was 60 years ago. It is rather a war of attrition which

Socialist Worker, 16 June 1973

suddenly flares up into large battles as one or another section of workers makes a breakthrough (the miners in 1972 and 1974, the dockers at the time of Pentonville). For a moment the need for unity becomes apparent, and then the struggle fragments again into small, piecemeal skirmishes.

For these reasons, building a mass rank and file movement will be very arduous and will demand a great deal of initiative and imagination to transcend sectional divisions in the working class while avoiding empty formalism – organizational shells substituting for real *action.*

That means mass meetings in every area – of engineers, teachers, gas workers, miners, civil servants, Ford workers, health workers – to plan united action. It means building solidly-based local committees that cut across sectional boundaries and create a real unity of purpose.

The new rank and file movement would have to forge a clear policy towards the trade union bureaucracy. The movement would have to make a decisive change: from putting pressure on the union leaders to action *in spite* of these leaders. The rank and file movement would have to raise hard and sharp the question: who owns the unions? And who should own them? Should they be the property of their 11 million members or of the tiny handful of union bureaucrats?

These questions will need to be translated into clear demands:
- **All strikes in support of trade union principles, conditions or wages to be made official.**
- **Dispute benefit to be raised by levy of entire membership when necessary.**
- **No secret negotiations with employers or government.**
- **Every stage of negotiations to be subject to rank and file ratification at mass meetings.**
- **All trade union officials to be elected and subject to instant recall.**

- All full-time officials to be paid the average wage in their industry.
- Union policy-making bodies to be made up from elected lay officers only.

Inflation plus unemployment bring the class struggle to the centre of political life, at a time when workers are better organized and more self-confident than ever before. Inflation, unemployment, to the accompaniment of the 'social contract', will raise for millions of workers the question of who gets what and why. Out of the coming struggles a new leadership will emerge from below. Socialism will come in from the cold.

9.
The Need to Build a Revolutionary Socialist Workers' Party

As the need grows to locate the industrial struggle in a political context, it becomes vital to know which political party workers could turn to as the vehicle for that struggle.

The Labour Party: withering of its working-class roots

The Labour Party of today is very different to what it was a generation or two ago. It has suffered a prolonged, irreversible decline in membership, and is now badly depopulated. How badly is shown in the careful study of the Labour Party in working-class Liverpool:

> At one ward meeting which I attended as an observer I was somehow counted twice and added to the six members present to make a quorum of eight – but only after I was asked if I had any objection to this procedure. In a number of other cases, ward parties which met only twice a year (once to re-elect ward officers and once to select a candidate) had very well-produced minutes of a further eight meetings.

> (B. Hindess, *The Decline of Working Class Politics,* London: McGibbon and Kee, 1971, p. 92)

Especially in the working-class areas, it has become a party of old people with longstanding membership:

Age and length of membership

Type of ward	Age	Membership
Middle-class area	43.6	13.9
Lower middle-skilled working-class area	50.4	19.8
Working-class area	46.5	21.6

(Hindess, p.93)

And it has become an inactive party, whose

> membership lists, where these exist, contain the names of people who are dead, have long since left the area, are no longer members and, in extreme cases, do not even know that they are in the party.
>
> (Hindess, p. 57)

Constituency parties throughout the country are slowly dying. Delegates cannot be found for conferences, General Management Committees shrivel and wards disappear; candidates cannot be found for local elections, and council Labour groups operate more and more as cliques independent of local parties.

Middle-class elements take over

The party is dying, leaving unfettered power in the hands of its professional organizers and the tiny groups of middle-class people — professionals and white-collar workers — who see in the party little more than a prop for the 'professionalized' and totally undemocratic cliques who run our large cities. In Liverpool, to continue with our example,

> all categories of manual workers are under-represented, the skilled workers least of all, while the professionals are the most over-represented.
>
> (Hindess, p. 61)

It is these professionals who determine local policies. This, in turn, 'affects both the number of local activists and the support for the party at both local and national elections' (Hindess, p. 120).

One should not draw the conclusion that in the more working-class communities, where middle-class elements are weaker, the Labour Party is stronger or healthier. Nothing of the sort. 'It is precisely in these areas that, from the point of view of its supporters, a strong and active party organization is hardly necessary' (Hindess, p. 131).

159

Death from boredom

Because the Labour Party is more and more divorced from real workers and real struggle, ward and General Management Committee meetings become increasingly empty and boring. At these meetings 60 to 70 per cent of the time spent is devoted to minutes, correspondence, reports of officers, reports of councillors, reports of delegates to other bodies, and administrative chores (Hindess, p. 70). Political discussion is limited and economic and industrial issues hardly ever mentioned. The party is truly dying at its roots.

The Parliamentary Labour Party and the Cabinet

The changes in the social composition of the Labour Party have been reflected in the parliamentary group:

After the 1951 election 37 per cent of Labour MPs came from working-class backgrounds; today not as many as 10 per cent do. The composition and educational background of the Parliamentary Labour Party elected in February 1974 is shown in the illustration on the next page.

The disappearance of former industrial workers has gone furthest in the Cabinet:

In Attlee's day half the Cabinet was made up of former manual workers; in Wilson's first Cabinet (1964) such people numbered 26 per cent; in his 1966 Cabinet, 17 per cent; in the reshuffle of 1967 it was down to 7 per cent; and in the reshuffle of October 1969 not one former manual worker remained. That old fraud Ray Gunter had a point when he said:

... to the ordinary fellow in the workshop, the Labour Party was *our party*. It was the instrument forged to help them in the pursuit of things that they thought were proper. The tragedy is that so many of the people in this country no longer think of it in that sense.

(*Listener*, 11 July 1968)

Labour Party Conferences — jamborees the leaders flout

One of the most unpleasant features of the Labour Party is its leadership's cynicism towards Annual Conference — the 'supreme body'.

To give one example, last year's Labour Party Conference, October 1973, passed a resolution calling for a ban on nuclear weapons in Britain and a cut of at least £1,000 million in military expenditure.

In January 1974, the National Executive Committee of the Labour Party and the Shadow Cabinet interpreted the

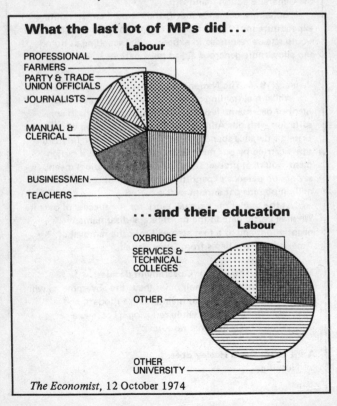

What the last lot of MPs did ...

Labour

PROFESSIONAL
FARMERS
PARTY & TRADE UNION OFFICIALS
JOURNALISTS
MANUAL & CLERICAL
BUSINESSMEN
TEACHERS

... and their education

Labour

OXBRIDGE
SERVICES & TECHNICAL COLLEGES
OTHER
OTHER UNIVERSITY

The Economist, 12 October 1974

Stages in watering the workers' resolutions

October 1973: The Labour Party Conference resolves:

'This conference welcomes all measures taken and planned to bring to an end the Cold War and believes Britain could make a tremendously significant contribution to the relaxation of world tension.

'To this end the Conference reaffirms last year's decision that it is opposed to any British defence policy which is based on the use or threatened use of nuclear weapons either by this country or its allies, demands the closing down of all nuclear bases, British and American, on British soil or in British waters and demands that this pledge be included in the General Election manifesto.

'Conference demands that Britain should cut its military expenditure initially by at least £1,000 millions per year. This would release resources to expand social spending at home and allow more generous aid to poor nations.'

January 1974: The National Executive Committee interprets:

'Whilst maintaining our support for NATO as an instrument of detente no less than of defence, we shall, in consultation with our Allies, progressively reduce the burden of Britain's defence spending to bring our costs into line with those carried by our main European allies. Such a realignment would, at present levels of defence spending, mean savings on defence expenditure by Britain of several hundred million pounds per annum over a period.

'At the same time we shall work for the success of detente. We shall participate in the multi-lateral-disarmament negotiations and as a first step will seek the removal of American Polaris bases from Great Britain.'

March 1974: The Labour Government decides:

'In conclusion with their allies they (the government) will pursue a policy directed to maintaining a modern and effective defence system while reducing its cost as a proportion of our national resources.'

April 1974: Denis Healey does:
Nothing.

resolution to mean that the American Polaris bases in Britain should be closed and that a few hundred million pounds ought to be lopped off the military budget 'over a period'.

But when the Queen's Speech was given in March 1974, the commitment had been still further watered down: no mention of nuclear weapons or bases, no figure for the cuts.

Lastly came Denis Healey's Budget in which a cut of £50 million was referred to. The Tories had gone further: in 1973 they cut the defence budget by £178 million!

The Labour leadership's cavalier attitude to Party Conference and even to the parliamentary Labour group is of long standing:

> The decision to manufacture the atom bomb was taken, according to the Minister of Defence at the time, Emanuel Shinwell, by the Prime Minister and Chiefs of Staff. The National Plan of 1965 was drawn up and announced without recourse to parliament or the Labour Party Conference. The multiple mergers between blocks of British industry have been permitted, often encouraged by the government, without recourse to parliamentary announcement or debate. The mass of statist councils, the National Economic Development Council (1961), the National Incomes and Prices Board (1965), the Industrial Reorganization Corporation (1966), the Commission for Industrial Relations (1968) and a host of others, have been taking decisions affecting the lives of millions of workers without so much as a debate in the House of Commons.
>
> (Paul Foot, 'Parliamentary Socialism' in N. Harris and J. Palmer, (eds.), *World Crisis*, London, 1969, p. 111)

Never again . . .

The Labour Party was not always so rotten. It was at one time rooted deeply in the working class. A couple of incidents from the life of George Lansbury are enough to show how different was the Labour Party of his time to what it is under Wilson.

On 1 September 1921, the Mayor of Poplar [George Lansbury],

and 29 other councillors went to prison for refusing to pay the sums due to the London County Council for purposes of local government, on the plea that the borough could not afford both to relieve the distresses of its own inhabitants and to meet these charges, which they held ought to fall upon the richer areas ...

The action of the Poplar Council in refusing to meet the precepts of the London County Council was followed in October by Stepney and Bethnal Green which were similarly in difficulties. Unemployed demonstrations in support of their attitude were broken up by the police; but on 12 October the Poplar councillors were released from prison, with the precept still unpaid.

(G. D. H. Cole, *A History of the Labour Party from 1914*, London, 1948, pp. 118-19)

Can one imagine Harold Wilson following George Lansbury? Breaking the law? Or going to prison in the interests of the unemployed?

In the second case, which happened a couple of years earlier, George Lansbury booked and paid for the Albert Hall in order to announce the decision to republish the *Herald* as a daily.

Hilton Carter, for the Council of the Hall, cancelled the letting arbitrarily and returned the money. An appeal to the government was in vain: 'It has no power whatever to intervene,' said Lloyd George. Then the Electrical Trades Union acted. It took out the fuses from the hall, and explained to the power-station manager that if he reconnected the place it would be obliged to put all Kensington in darkness. The hall tried to carry on with a glimmering sort of emergency light. But a great Victory Ball was in the offing, and the Licensed Vehicle Workers and other unions were arranging that no buses should stop at the hall, no taxis take customers to or away from it, and no electric trains stop either at South Kensington or High Street. The government which had 'no power whatever' to intervene, acted hastily ('Could Mr Lansbury possibly make it convenient to come round to the Board of Trade at once?'), instructed Hilton Carter, and Mr Lansbury had not one but two great meetings for his announcement.

(R. Postgate, *The Life of George Lansbury*, London, 1951, p. 184)

How could Wilson follow in Lansbury's footsteps? He does not know any power workers or busmen. He is too respectable to break the law of the land.

No Golden Age

Although it was better at one time than it is now, the Labour Party was never a *real socialist party*. Nor was it ever thought to be by the militants of the day at any stage in its history. Reviewing the first years of the Parliamentary Labour Party in his pamphlet *Is the Parliamentary Party a Failure?* (1908), Ben Tillett, leader of the 1889 dock strike, denounced the parliamentary leaders as 'sheer hypocrites' who 'for ten and five guineas a time will lie with the best' and who repaid 'with gross betrayal the class that willingly supports them' (Quoted in Ralph Miliband, *Parliamentary Socialism*, London, 1961, p. 28).

The atmosphere in parliament had always exercized a strong corroding effect on the socialist morale of Labour M Ps.

David Kirkwood, one of the 'wild men', wrote later that, before he entered the House of Commons in 1922, he knew little of 'the Great Ones, the Powerful Ones, the Lordly Ones' but felt that 'they and the world they represented were crushing my fellows down into poverty, misery, despair and death'. When he entered the House, however, he found that 'it was full of wonder. I had to shake myself occasionally as I found myself moving about and talking with men whose names were household words. More strange it was to find them all so simple and unaffected and friendly'. Violently attacked over unemployment, Bonar Law 'showed no resentment' and expressed pleasure at hearing Kirkwood's Glasgow accent; denounced as a 'Uriah Heep', Stanley Baldwin, the Chancellor of the Exchequer, was gently reproachful and thus 'pierced a link in my armour that had never been pierced before'; and a Conservative member, having heard Kirkwood make a 'flaming speech' about the poverty of crofters in the Hebrides, told him, so the latter records in wonder, 'I could not vote for you, but I should like to help those men if I may,' and gave him a £5 note.

(Quoted by Miliband, pp. 95-96)

It was the ministers of the first Labour government (1923-24) who reached the greatest depths of submission to their 'betters'. Stephen Walsh, the Minister of War, was supposed to have told the generals: 'I know my place. You have commanded armies in the field when I was nothing but a private in the ranks.' Another account has it that he opened the first meeting of the Army Council with the words: 'Gentlemen, always remember that we must all be loyal to the King.' J. H. Thomas, the new Colonial Secretary, was said to have introduced himself to the heads of departments at the Colonial Office with the statement, 'I am here to see that there is no mucking about with the British Empire.' Beatrice Webb describes in her diary a gay luncheon party at which 'we were all laughing over Wheatley — the revolutionary — going down on both knees and actually kissing the King's hand'. She also noted that 'Uncle Arthur [Henderson] was bursting with childish joy over his H O seals in the red leather box which he handed round the company'.

In office, the Labour Party has always ensured the continuity of the capitalist state and guarded its harshest, most anti-working-class plans:

When the railway workers struck in 1919 an elaborate emergency supply and transport system was worked out under the control of Sir Eric Geddes, at that time Minister of Transport. This system was not fully tested at the time, and in the following years it lapsed almost completely. In 1923 the task of revising it was put into the hands of J. C. C. Davidson, Chancellor of the Duchy of Lancaster. A groundwork had been laid, no more, when the first Labour government came to power, and Davidson, handing over to Josiah Wedgwood, asked him not to destroy what had been done ... When ... the Labour government went out of office and Wedgwood handed over again to Davidson, he said: 'I haven't destroyed any of your plans. In fact I haven't done a bloody thing about them.' The plan remained a skeleton until Red Friday taught the government a lesson.

(J. Symons, *The General Strike*, London, 1957, pp. 23-24)

These emergency supply and transport schemes were used a couple of years later against the General Strike.

One of the worst indictments of the Labour Party leadership is its behaviour towards the unemployed during the second Labour government (1929-31).

> In their evidence before the Blanesburgh Committee on Unemployment Insurance in 1926, the T U C and the Labour Party had jointly proposed an increased scale of unemployment benefits of 20s a week, with 10s for a dependent wife and 5s for each child, and 'to that scale it adheres', *Labour and the Nation* had said. That these pledges would be fulfilled must have been the expectation of many who had voted for the return of a Labour government in 1929.
>
> However, when the government introduced its Unemployment Insurance Bill in November 1929, the Bill was found to leave the unemployment benefit for men at 17s a week, and the allowance for each child at 2s; only the allowance of the wife was raised from 7s to 9s, and the benefits for unemployed juvenile workers were also slightly increased.
>
> (Miliband, p. 164)

Change in the functioning of the Labour Party

For a very long period the prevailing ideology of the British working class was that of parliamentary reformism, a 'reformism from above' which more or less told workers: 'Leave it to your leaders – your M Ps and your trade union chiefs – to win reforms for you'.

It was not an unrealistic policy in its time. All through the nineteenth and well into the twentieth centuries the typical employer was a great deal smaller than he is today. And the market in which he sold his goods was extremely competitive. He could not on the whole afford to pay his workers more, or grant them greater concessions, than his competitors. Nor did he have much incentive to do so. Also, the level of unemployment was normally high at this stage in the development of capitalism and labour was easily available. It was also fairly mobile, since, to a greater extent than today, workers' skills (or lack of skills) were transferable between factories and industries. As a result, when the employers were forced to grant reforms to the workers, they tended to do so all together and all at once, through parliament. And it was through national agitation and pressure focused on parliament and channelled through representatives (or misrepresentatives!) that workers made many of their gains.

The nineteenth and early twentieth century state fitted the strategy of parliamentary reformism very well. By and large, the state kept out of economic life. Despite the misery and poverty caused by fierce competition, and by recurrent heavy unemployment, it made sure that the parties to contracts kept to their bargains, and no more. Insofar as it was possible, politics and economics were kept strictly separate.

In the circumstances it was not unreasonable for workers to see the state as being somehow 'neutral', above the conflict between workers and employers. It was also not unreasonable to believe that if only the representatives of the working class could be elected to parliament in large enough numbers, these representatives could then legislate their way to socialism and a just society.

All this has changed fundamentally.

The state and big business have drawn closer together. Private capitalism, aided by nationalized industries that are run by a capitalist state on capitalist lines in the interests of capitalism, has demanded a new central managing role from the government. And the state is a major business in its own right.

The result is that the state can no longer be thought of as neutral between workers and employers. It is the biggest employer. The Labour Party can no longer be thought of as a party of reforms. It is a party of management of capitalism. Besides, business is bigger and less competitive than it was and so much more vulnerable to direct pressure from workers – to reformism from below – and more able to meet their demands.

The working class too has changed. Workers are better off than ever in the past. They are more confident and more self-directed. They are fighting for better wages, fighting in defence of their shop stewards and fighting for their right to control the conditions of work. They are fighting for themselves, directly, and not leaving it to their leaders, and in the process, they are destroying the tradition of reformism from above. A new tradition of 'do-it-yourself' reformism is emerging.

No wonder workers are indifferent towards parliament. They know, or if they don't know they can easily believe, that Labour M Ps spoke 200,000 words against the Industrial Relations Bill (Act) without upsetting Heath in the slightest; but that the smile was wiped clean off his face by the dockers when they struck to free their five mates! Socialists need not worry about this indifference; we'd have more cause to worry if workers *did* show an interest in parliament.

Workers also remember Labour's record of reforms: for instance, that the 1964-70 Wilson government put means-testing (politely called selectivity) at the centre of its policies for the social services; that it legislated in the concept of 'fair rents'; that it pioneered the abolition of free milk for school children; that its housing record was abysmal; that it tried to bring in anti-union laws; that it slavishly followed U S foreign policy and endorsed every atrocity Johnson and then Nixon inflicted on Vietnam.

There never was a parliamentary road to socialism. There was, however, a parliamentary road to real and significant reforms under massive extra-parliamentary pressure. Today that road does not exist.

Both the Tories and Labour are committed to managing capitalism. They share a consensus about politics that has become more and more pronounced over the last 20 years and more appalling as its centre of gravity shifts to the right. Take, for instance, the question of immigration control. In 1958 when Oswald Mosley fought a parliamentary by-election on a platform of immigration control he was opposed by Tories, Liberals and Labour. When in 1963 the Tories introduced controls on black immigration, Gaitskell, the right-wing leader of the Labour Party, was most vehement in denouncing it. Yet one of the first acts of the Wilson government was to limit black Commonwealth immigrants. *Immigration from the Commonwealth,* a White Paper published August 1965, which cut the number of entrants to 8,500 a year, shamelessly underwrote all the arguments of racialists, particularly that shortages in housing, schools and hospitals were in some way aggravated by immigrants. More scandalous still was the Commonwealth Immigration Act of February 1968 which 'controlled' the entry of Asians from Kenya who had been promised free entry by a former Conservative government. Labour's failure to combat the campaigns for immigration control created a political vacuum smartly occupied by Enoch Powell, who in a single speech in April 1968 demolished all the liberal endeavour of the previous two years and set race relations back further than they had ever been before.

The Tory-Labour consensus covers most things. In the field of labour relations it is almost uncanny, as anyone who has read both Barbara Castle's 'In Place of Strife' and Robert Carr's Industrial Relations Act will know.

No wonder fewer people see much difference between Labour and the Tories. In 1951 the opinion polls reported that only 20 per cent of the electorate thought there was 'nothing to choose' between the two major parties. In 1964 the percentage had grown to 49. In 1971 the figure was 55 per cent.

Clearly, the mass of electors are more and more indifferent and apathetic. Two million people who voted in the February 1974 general election did not vote again in

October. Politicians and the media described the October election as the most important one this century. Yet the turnout at the polls was down from 78 per cent in February to 72 per cent. Fewer people voted Labour than in any other election since the war. Fewer than in 1959, when Labour lost the election by more than 100 seats; fewer even than in 1945, when there were eight million fewer votes than today.

Labour Party votes cast

	Number (thousands)	Per cent
1929	8,380	36.6
1931	6,648	30.0
1935	8,460	38.5
1945	11,992	48.0
1950	13,296	46.4
1951	13,948	48.7
1955	12,405	46.3
1959	12,216	43.8
1964	12,206	44.1
1966	13,066	47.9
1970	12,179	42.9
1974 (Feb)	11,647	37.2
1974 (Oct)	11,459	39.6

Labour has gained its tiny majority not because it enthused the electorate with its policies, but because the Tory vote splintered. More than five million people — most of them Tory sympathizers, voted Liberal. Nearly a million Scots — a third of the adult population — voted for the Nationalists. Labour actually polled fewer votes than in any election since 1945.

The Communist Party

One might have expected the Communist Party to have benefited from the erosion of Labour Party support among workers. But nothing of the sort has happened.

The Communist Party's electoral performance has been frightful:

Communist Party vote

	Number	Votes per CP candidate
1945	102,780	4,894
1950	91,736	917
1951	21,600	2,164
1955	33,144	1,950
1959	38,897	1,716
1964	44,567	1,236
1966	62,112	1,088
1970	38,431	663
1974 (Feb)	32,741	774
1974 (Oct)	17,426	601

In October 1974 the party took a terrible drubbing. All 29 deposits were lost, including that of Jimmy Reid in Dunbartonshire, who saved his deposit last time. Reid got 3,417 votes compared with 5,928 before.

In almost every constituency where Communist candidates stood, their vote was badly down on the already pathetic February total. In some places, the vote was halved. The total Communist vote — 17,426 — was the lowest the party has registered since 1931.

The strategy which set the Communist Party on this dismal course was presented in *The British Road to Socialism* issued by the Executive Committee in February 1951 and revised and adopted by the Twenty-second Congress in April 1952. It is basically a reformist strategy characterized by parliamentary cretinism, a reliance on the Labour Party, and an abject kow-towing to the 'left' trade union bureaucracy.

Many years ago the programme of the Communist International made clear what a revolutionary workers' movement would do to the capitalist state:

> The conquest of power by the proletariat is the violent over-throw of bourgeois power, the destruction of the capitalist state apparatus (bourgeois armies, police, bureaucratic hierarchy, the judiciary, parliaments, etc.) and the substitution in its place of new organs of proletarian power.

In contrast *The British Road to Socialism* suggests some changes in personnel and this only at the top. Nowhere does it argue for the destruction of the capitalist state. Nowhere is there discussion of the need to establish workers' councils, of a workers' militia to replace the standing army, or a workers' anything. Instead we are offered:

> Persisting through every change of government are the heads of the armed forces, the police, the security network, the top civil servants in the main ministries, the judges, the controllers of the nationalized industries . . .
>
> The leading positions in the ministries and departments, the armed forces and the police, the nationalized industries and other authorities must, therefore, be filled by men and women loyal to socialism . . . this ensures that the socialist policies determined on by parliament are fully implemented.
>
> (*The British Road to Socialism,* third edition, 1968, pp. 10, 38)

And how should industry be run? Not a word about workers' control over production. The section on 'Industrial Democracy' begins with a plea for workers' participation. And even this tired old Liberal demand is justified in a very apologetic tone:

> These are justifiable demands. The right of the workers to be involved in policy making and control in industry is essential for economic advance and to safeguard the interests of the working people.
>
> (p. 33)

What about the nationalized industries? Even here no talk of workers' control or management:

In nationalized industries the trade unions should be directly represented on national boards and at all levels of management — and at workshop and plant level the workers should have rights of consultation and participation in all management decisions.
(p. 33)

Consultation! Not even the power of veto is suggested! From this reformist, parliamentary hash follows naturally a policy of 'unity' with all and sundry, even church bodies. Thus the 1958 edition of the *British Road* suggested that

A united labour movement . . . would win the support of men and women and young people who are at present not associated with Labour but who are striving for progressive social aims and a better life through tenants' and residents' associations, youth organizations, women's institutes, British Legion sections, church organizations and many other national and local bodies of this kind. It would win the support of many professional workers, small farmers and business people who now support the Tories.
(pp. 29-30)

The 1968 edition of the *British Road* makes it clear that the Communist Party's aim in life is to become the left echo of the Labour Party:

Contrary to the ideas spread by some Labour leaders it is not the aim of the Communist Party to undermine, weaken or split the Labour Party.
(p. 24)

What then is the aim of the C P? The answer: to reform the Labour Party.

As Communists we sincerely desire the strengthening of the left trends within the Labour Party. We believe that the struggle of the socialist forces to make it a party of action and socialism will grow and that the growth of the Communist Party will help this development. When the Labour Party rejects reformism, moves into the attack on capitalism, ends the bans and proscriptions against the left, it will ensure itself a vital role in the building of

socialism.
(p. 24)

For a long time the main industrial strategy of the C P has been to win official positions in the trade union hierarchy. With the increasing integration of the union bureaucracy with the state and its ideological justification under Labour, the irrelevance of C P policies is bound to increase.

C P policies are being undermined from another direction too. For decades it used to get a new infusion of blood from thousands of industrial workers who in practice cared less for trade union elections than for plant militancy. Many of them were to all intents and purposes less interested in the C P as a *political* organization, than as a community of industrial militants. The majority of C P members in industry for many years have been really pure syndicalists. With the encroachment in the shop of general issues — incomes policy, legislation to emasculate the shop stewards, etc. — the co-existence of syndicalist tactics and political reformism is undermined. Every time a general issue is raised, the C P members in industry are split from top to bottom. During the anti-Devlin strike in 1967, C P dockers in Southampton supported Devlin and scabbed. So did Lindley, the C P leader of the lightermen in London. Will Paynter's policy of no resistance to closures and attacks on absenteeism split the C P miners, and so on.

More recently, Eddy Marsden, General Secretary of the constructional section of the A U E W and C P Executive member, signed a letter, jointly with D. J. Gorman (construction manager, Simon Litwin Ltd), stating that the Simon Litwin's Llandarcy site was 'now open for recruitment for A U E W construction section riggers and erectors' while 57 construction workers were locked out by management (reported in *Socialist Worker,* 25 March 1972).

As for the C P's attitude to the 'left' trade union leaders, their reporting of Jack Jones' speech to the Scottish

Conference of the T & G W U in Motherwell on 17 October 1974 illustrates it neatly. The *Financial Times* described the speech as 'a strong appeal to union members to tone down wage demands and improve industrial relations'. The *Guardian* described it as 'sweet music for the government ... from the lips of Mr Jack Jones ... when he issued a call for workers to observe some kind of wage restraint'. The *Morning Star,* however, was far more flattering to Jack Jones. It headlined its report: 'Raise Real Wages to Fight Inflation Says Jack Jones'.

The malaise in the C P is clear enough. Its unashamedly parliamentary approach has increased the irritation and despair among many fine party militants who do not want to devote their time and energy to electioneering, when there is less and less to show for it. Many party members are not even readers, let alone sellers, of the *Morning Star.* The party plays a more and more routine bureaucratic role. Its incapacity to mobilize its own members for any campaign is unbelievable.

The C P is too tired to be shocked. Even when its 'parliamentary road' received a blow from the bloody disintegration of an identical electoral strategy in Chile, its reaction was short and shallow. The recent news of C P involvement with the military rulers in Portugal, following practically the same path as Allende did in Chile, caused not a whisper of debate in the British C P.

The need for a really socialist revolutionary workers' party

For generations millions of workers believed that the economic or trade union struggle was separate from the political struggle. When they wanted improvements in wages or conditions of work they joined a trade union. When they wanted to bring about more general, political changes they looked towards the Labour Party.

But the harsh reality of the last few years has hammered this concept of the separation of politics from economics into the ground. Politics invades every corner of the life of working people. When they demand a wage rise they meet not only the resistance of the employer but also that of the government. Rent – the Housing Finance Act – was politics. Prices are politics. The Industrial Relations Act was politics.

The employing class uses two weapons to exploit and oppress working people the economic one and the political one.

To fight back, workers need to use their industrial power not only against individual employers but against the organization of the employing class as a whole – government.

Where does the power of workers lie? It cannot lie in the ballot box. Big business does not abide by the decisions of the parliamentary vote. Was it parliament that allowed Lonrho to transfer thousands of pounds to the Cayman Islands? Is it parliament that dictates the production pricing and plans of the multinational companies?

Where workers are concerned, the ballot box shows not their real power but their impotence. For working people, general elections give an opportunity to mark a cross against a candidate's name. If the average person lives to the age of 70 and elections take place every five years, it means that he or she will, at best, mark ten crosses. Marking a cross does not take very long – say a minute for a really slow writer. That means ten minutes of democracy in a lifetime. Ten minutes is not very much democracy or very much popular power.

In parliamentary terms dockers have much less power than shopkeepers – after all there are 20 times more shopkeepers than dockers in the country. But in industrial terms the dockers are incomparably more powerful. It was they, through industrial action, that freed the Pentonville Five, and shook Heath.

But spontaneous action like that is not enough to bring about socialism. Without a revolutionary party there can be no victorious working-class revolution.

Revolutions do indeed start as spontaneous acts. The French revolution started with the storming of the Bastille. Nobody organized it. There was no party at the head of the uprising. Even the future Jacobin leaders like Robespierre did not yet oppose the monarchy, nor were they yet organized into a party. The revolution on 14 July 1789 was a spontaneous act of the masses.

The same is true of the Russian revolutions of 1905 and of February 1917. The 1905 revolution started with a bloody clash between the Tsar's army and police and a mass of workers – men, women and children – led by a priest (and agent provocateur) Gapon. The workers were far from being organized by a clear decisive leadership with a socialist policy of its own. Carrying icons, they came to beg their beloved 'little Father' – the Tsar – to help them against their exploiters. Twelve years later, in February 1917, the masses, this time more experienced, and among whom there were a greater number of socialists, again rose spontaneously. No historian has been able to point a finger at the organizer of the February revolution; it was simply not organized.

However, after being triggered spontaneously, revolutions move forward in a different way. In France, the transition from the semi-republican government of the Gironde to the revolutionary government which annihilated feudal property relations, was not carried out by unorganized masses without party leadership, but under the decisive leadership of the Jacobin Party. Without such a party this important step, which demanded an all-out fight against the Girondists, would have been impossible. The people of Paris could, spontaneously and leaderless, rise up against the king, after decades of oppression. But they were too conservative in the main, too lacking in historical experience and knowledge, to distinguish, after only two or three years, between those who wanted to drive the revolution forward to its limit, and those who aimed at some compromise. A bitter struggle was required against the party of compromise, the allies of yesterday. The conscious leadership of this great undertaking was supplied by the Jacobin Party. It fixed the date (10 August 1792) and organized the overthrow of the Gironde down to the last detail.

Nor was the October revolution a spontaneous act. It was organized in practically all its important particulars, including the date, by the Bolsheviks. During the zigzags of revolution between February and October — the June demonstration, the July days and subsequent orderly retreat, the defeat of the Kornilov putsch, and so on — the workers and soldiers came more closely under the influence and guidance of the Bolshevik Party, until the time came for it to press the revolution to final victory.

As against this, the events of May 1968 in Paris showed clearly that while a few hundred students or workers can build a barricade, to overthrow the capitalist regime and seize state power, a much larger centralized organization is necessary.

If only the workers in Paris in 1968 had remembered the experience of Paris in 1936, or of the Italian workers in 1920! If only they had had a revolutionary party, for such a party is also the memory of the class, the store of experience of class struggle internationally.

The ruling class is easily able to organize its affairs according to a coherent strategy. It is itself highly centralized, with a massive state apparatus at its disposal, many newspapers, massive research organizations.

If militant workers are going to win the arguments with their workmates and counter the plans of big business, then they have to be organized as well. They have to be able to refute every piece of employers' propaganda with arguments of their own, and to suggest tactics that will lead to unity and victory every time the employers try to divide the workers.

None of this is possible without a revolutionary party, linking together the most militant workers in every factory, mine and office. Through such an organization, militants can develop the experience of working together and of relating every struggle to the overall aim of overthrowing capitalism.

Facing the strictly centralized and disciplined power of the capitalists there must be a no less centralized and disciplined fighting organization of the proletariat.

Because of the instability built into capitalism, there are going to be many sharp changes in objective economic conditions. Because these changes do not find immediate expression in the consciousness and activity of the class, impeded as they are by tradition and by reformist organization, we must expect many turns in the struggle, from economic strikes to political battles and vice-versa; from semi-revolutionary situations to reaction; from lulls to mass strikes whose scope and temper is insurrectionary. The unevenness in experience and activity between sections of the class, between different factories and industries, is going to continue, with sometimes a levelling up, and sometimes a levelling down, and always an upset of whatever equilibrium is achieved.

What is necessary under such conditions is a revolutionary organization that is able not only to distinguish between a revolutionary situation and a counter-revolutionary one — this is quite easy — but between all the nuances in the intermediate stages between them, an organization stringent in its principles, yet highly adaptable and elastic in its tactics, and always aware of the sharp turns in the situation.

There is growing awareness among militants that politics is not something that can be left to the ballot box and the

Tweedledum-Tweedledee Tory and Labour Parties. It is now possible to talk, and talk credibly, of the need to build a socialist workers' party that will sweep away capitalism. Building such a party is now fully on the agenda. It is a challenge the International Socialists willingly accept.

Such a party has its mainspring in workplace branches. That is where workers' power lies. And that is why last year I S built 38 factory branches and this year the I S Conference decided to aim at 80 factory branches plus a number of white-collar branches by autumn 1975.

In every place of work the real socialists are few in number. They are isolated and naturally often feel depressed and moody. Frequently one socialist militant does not even know others who share the same views and attitudes. **The I S branch will aim to bring them together.**

In every large workplace there is a tiny minority of scabs at one extreme and a tiny group of militant socialists at the other. In between stands the big majority — not right-wing but simply uninformed and conservative. **The I S factory branch, with the help of leaflets, bulletins and the rank and file papers relevant to the industry, will try to influence that majority of workers.**

Third, **the I S branch in the factory will plan the local adaptation and execution of policies laid down by the national organization.** This could mean for example, gaining a pledge for solidarity strikes with any worker fighting the 'social contract'.

Fourth, **the I S branch will hold regular meetings to plan how best they might express and represent the interests of the workers in the factory.**

Fifth, **the I S branch will hold regular political meetings to discuss current events and socialist theory, as featured in the organization's press and publications.**

There are many thousands of workers who buy *Socialist Worker* regularly in many large places of work. It is their duty to join us in the effort to build factory branches.

It is quite obvious that revolutionaries in Britain are weak at present. They are small in number, split into a number of groupings, often isolated because of their social composition, and above all lacking experience in leading mass struggles. But these weaknesses can be overcome. Readiness to learn, readiness to experiment systematically, above all readiness to try and translate general theories into practical activity, this is what is necessary. In a complex and rapidly changing situation, readiness to move from simple tasks to more difficult ones, above all readiness to overcome one's own mistakes, is crucial. 'The fighting party of the advanced class need not fear mistakes. What it should fear is persistence in mistakes, refusal to admit and correct the mistakes. . .' (Lenin).

In this period of rapid change, there is a danger that revolutionaries will drag behind the movement of the class. There is only one way of dealing with that: by building a strong revolutionary organization, with branches in the factories, pits, docks and offices, so that tactical demands are not arrived at arbitrarily by isolated militants, but reached through discussion by workers with a shared perspective. The key thing in the coming period is the ability to shift rapidly from one demand to another as the situation changes — from defence to offence, from economic to political demands and back again. Besides initiative and perseverance, the rootedness of revolutionaries will be at a special premium.

Revolutionary socialists will have to combine the most meticulous persistence in all the battles of the working class side by side with recruitment to the organization. We have to face the fact that there is a yawning abyss between the greatness of the task facing us and the *actual* poverty of our movement. We need to bridge this abyss.

Above all, through factory and workplace organization the revolutionary socialist party will counter to the twisted priorities of capitalism the socialist planned economy.

10.
Socialist Planned Economy

We have to react to the crisis at a number of levels. First of all we have to resist the attempt to load it on to the workers' shoulders. Workers must defend their standard of living to strengthen their confidence, their morale, their organization, their socialist consciousness. Secondly we have to emphasize in argument and propaganda that the crisis flows from the logic of capitalism itself. And thirdly we must make it absolutely clear that there is an alternative to capitalism – the socialist planned economy.

The anarchy of capitalism

If all the shareholders, bankers, and the whole of the City of London sank without trace, the output of the factories could only go up, for the existence of these creatures is a terrible impediment to increasing production. Unfortunately, we won't have such luck. The owners of property are not going to disappear just like that. They are not going to give up their wealth and power without the bitterest of struggles.

When the government, the employers, the press and television talk of efficiency, *socialists should have plenty to say about the anarchy and waste of capitalist production:* the fact that more is spent on advertising than on basic research; that millions of pounds are spent on armaments; that constant retooling of car plants takes place, not because the tools are worn out, but because competition demands accelerated obsolescence and never-ending new models. When one takes a look at the criminal anarchy and waste of capitalist production, the appeal to workers to raise production is just a farce.

At least one million people who would like to work do not work – the registered unemployed plus those unregistered. If they produced on average the same as employed people are producing at present, the total addition to the national income would be about £3,000 million a year – about £4 a week extra for a family of four.

Again, look at the total national income, and ask what would happen if production took place without stop-go, recessions and slump. In 1973 the Gross National Product was £56,259 million. Had this been shared out equally it would have meant an income of more than £4,000 per year – about £80 per week for every family of four, enough to eliminate poverty in the country. But how much could we have produced had we all worked steadily, had we all used currently available techniques – nothing fancy or ultra-new, just what is currently available – had we used the skill of all the people to the full, year in and year out? We can't know exactly but we can make a rough guess. Over the years 1951 to 1973, the Gross National Product in Britain rose 2.5 per cent per year on average. Had the rate of growth been instead 6 per cent – not a very high rate compared with capitalist Japan – the Gross National Product in 1973 would have been not £56,259 million but £112,700 million. This could have meant an *increase* of £4,000 for every family of four, so that the average annual income per family in 1973 would have been over £8,000.

Or take a specific sector of the economy – housing – and calculate simply what the situation would have been had Wilson's promise of 500,000 houses a year been realized. It is not a very high target; it has been beaten, relative to their populations, by West Germany, France, Holland and Denmark; and it is not very ambitious compared with the need. Yet if we had reached it between 1951 and 1973 there would have been 4,091,264 more new houses than existed at the end of 1973.

Waste

Waste under capitalism takes many, many forms. It has really terrifying dimensions. A library of volumes will not suffice to describe them. For lack of space we shall have to make do with very few examples.

First of all — military expenditure, the most criminal of all wastes. At £78,397 million in the last 27 years, it amounts to £5,600 for every family of four!

Britain: military expenditure 1948 — 1974 (in £ million)

Year	£ million	Year	£ million
1948	1,884	1961	2,895
1949	1,930	1962	2,976
1950	2,071	1963	3,001
1951	2,602	1964	3,056
1952	3,271	1965	3,085
1953	3,362	1966	3,113
1954	3,250	1967	3,319
1955	3,092	1968	3,211
1956	3,152	1969	2,860
1957	2,905	1970	2,890
1958	2,708	1971	2,965
1959	2,754	1972	3,097
1960	2,816	1973	3,082

| 1974 | 3,050 (Government estimate) |

from: National Income and Expenditure Blue Books

Another source of fantastic waste is the misdirection of potential investment. So long as there is profit, a capitalist does not care if it comes from production or speculation. Result? In the three years of Barber boom 1971-73, no less than £4,000 million poured into speculation in land and office building in London alone.

Nor do the capitalists care where the profit comes from — Britain or abroad. In recent years there has been a massive export of capital (see table opposite).

Capital Exports from Britain
(in £ million)

1963	320	1968	727
1964	399	1969	679
1965	368	1970	773
1966	303	1971	875
1967	456	1972	1,450
		1973	1,253

from: *National Institute Economic Review, May 1974*, p.96

The attractions of investing abroad are obvious. As the South African government tells it:

> Capital investment in South Africa yields one of the highest returns in the world and is an area well worth further investigation.

(Advertisement in *The Banker*, October 1973)

In 1970 and 1971 profits per worker at the Leyland Motor Corporation of South Africa were about five times higher than profits per worker in British Leyland (Counter Information Services, *British Leyland: The Beginning of the End?*, London, 1973, p. 34). And no wonder; a report in the *Guardian* (12 March 1972) explains:

> According to the International Metal Workers' Federation, which visited South Africa last year, some African workers at Leyland's Blackheath plant are being paid less than £5 (R9.75) per week. Mr Peter Noble, Leyland's personnel manager, declined to comment. 'This is the Republic of South Africa, whether you like it or not', he said. 'I personally am anti-press. I have had too much trouble with you lot buggering up labour relations.'

Turn to oil. A study of the American economy by Michael Kidron and Elana Gluckstein concludes that no less than 57 per cent of U S oil and gas consumption is by waste industries. The most significant waste industry is the military sector, which absorbed 10.7 per cent of oil and gas output. Another 15.5 per cent went on such non-productive activities as advertising, finance, insurance, real estate, rental and business services. On top of this was to be added the consumption of those who perform various policing and 'law-enforcing' operations for the capitalist system – both as policemen and supervisors in industry. These added 18.3 per cent to the total waste of oil ('Waste: The U S 1970' in Michael Kidron, *Capitalism and Theory,* Pluto Press, 1974).

But capitalism is wasteful in a wider sense even than could be considered in that study. Massive waste occurs even in the 'productive' sector of the economy – when goods that could go by rail go by road, or when workers are compelled to drive their individual cars to work through the inadequacy of public transport.

Then take the insulting waste that we are supposed to put up with cheerfully: The investiture of Prince Charles in 1969 cost £½ million, not counting the cost of police, soldiers, civil servants, and flunkeys. It is thought that the final total for one day's royal fun and games was close on £1 million. That sort of money could have been put to better use in Wales which had 40,000 unemployed at the time and where 31 per cent of the houses are more than 80 years old. £30,000 was spent on temporary toilets for the day; in Wales 37,000 houses have no inside toilets, 1,840 have no bathrooms.

Besides these large-scale sources of waste, every worker knows from experience how costly capitalist mismanagement is at work. A docker wrote to me:

There are many occasions when gangs are allocated to jobs when the ship doesn't even arrive. There have been occasions when gangs have been allocated to a hatch on the ship, opened the hatch and found no cargo. There are more stoppages due to the employers not having barges ready for the discharging operations than all the strikes combined in dockland. Many disputes are caused by sending 11 men to a job which by custom and practice has always been a 12-handed operation, while at the same time the employer has sent home men unemployed on full back-pay.

A London busman wrote to me:

It's crazy. The more desperately they try to save money, the greater the waste and chaos they create. Due to their failure to pay enough wages there is a desperate shortage of conductors — and as a result in this shed there are drivers who haven't turned a wheel for weeks and buses that haven't carried a passenger for as long. As a result the bus queues grow longer and the loss in wasted time must be fantastic. Why can't they make the only really worthwhile economy by cutting out fares altogether and run the buses as a service — save millions on fare collection, security, accounting, checking and banking — and at the same time provide a quicker, better and more reliable service to the public? I'd call that real productivity.

A worker in a large engineering factory in North London wrote:

We found, in the scrapyard, several hundred expensive electrical components for cars. They were checked and found to be in order. So we helped ourselves. We later found that it was cheaper for management to scrap these parts than to store them in the warehouse.

(T. Cliff, *The Employers' Offensive,* Pluto Press, 1970, pp. 153-55).

Things can only be different with the ending of capitalist power.

Realizing people's potentialities

One of capitalism's worst crimes is the way it stunts the creative ability and suppresses the intellectual development of people by a deadening routine of work. Marx described the effect on workers of the capitalist method of production in this way:

Intelligence in production expands in one direction because it vanishes in many others. What is lost by the detail labourers, is concentrated in the capital that employs them. It is a result of the division of labour in manufactures, that the labourer is brought face to face with the intellectual potencies of the material process of production, as the property of another, and as a ruling power.

(Karl Marx, *Capital,* vol. 1, pp. 396-97)

From its earliest days capitalism has tried to make of workers mere raw material in the productive process. In the capitalist economy the worker is an object, merchandise, and the capitalist treats him as such. The worker is not seen as a human being entitled to live his or her own life, but as labour power, a possible source of profit. Even if workers resist these pressures, so long as capitalism exists, they are robbed of their fantastic creative ability, of their deepest nature.

A socialist planned economy will free the productive forces from relative stagnation, for as Marx put it, 'Of all the instruments of production, the greatest productive power is the revolutionary class itself.'

The largest increase in output will result from the socialist reorganization of the factories. At present most work is reduced to uncreative routine. Freeing the creative abilities of all workers in the factory in an atmosphere of trust and co-operation would have effects beyond the imagination. 'Only the masses', said Lenin, 'can really plan, for they alone are everywhere.' Management by an exploiting class is intrinsically always irrational, because it is always external to the productive activity itself. An exploiting class can at best have only a fragmented knowledge of the real conditions in which production takes place.

Crucial to socialist planning is the full development of every individual's potentialities, his or her conscious and voluntary participation in a productive process which is no longer felt to be alien.

The international framework of socialism

But if the factories, mines, docks – the apparatus of production – were nationalized without compensation and run under workers' control, would not the whole enterprise be paralyzed by the flight of capital?

Under capitalism a flight of money capital does affect production. But when the capitalists are expropriated it does not matter in the least if they export their money capital, their bank balances. They will be exporting bits of paper. Production is not concerned with bits of paper, but with machines, railways, factories, mines; and the capitalists cannot pinch a mine, or a factory, and export it.

But what about a blockade of socialist Britain? The truth is that 'socialism in one country' is not on, particularly in a country as dependent for raw materials and food as Britain. So is socialism doomed in Britain? Should we wait with folded arms until workers make the revolution in other countries?

The danger for the revolution from national isolation is a very serious one. The Russian people paid dearly for it in Stalinism, with its lack of freedom, its one-man management in the factories, its denial of the right to strike, its fantastic privileges for the few combined with deprivation for the many.

But we need not expect a British revolution to be isolated. The British economy is totally integrated into the international economy of the Western capitalist countries. Its heartbeat is in perfect timing with theirs. The same scourges of inflation, stagnation, afflict them all. International capitalism has made the world a small place. It has become a small place for workers too.

The integration of workers' struggle is spreading far and wide. Workers at British Leyland here should have acted in solidarity with workers employed by Leyland in Spain and Chile. Plessey workers here and in Portugal, Pilkington workers here and in Chile — their need to act together becomes more urgent as it becomes more possible.

After the revolution in Britain, the B B C (perhaps renamed the Workers' Revolutionary Broadcasting Station) could carry out a very simple appeal to workers around the world: Take into your own hands former British capital. Black workers of South Africa! With your sweat and blood you created the gold mines. They are yours! Workers throughout the world — take!

An appeal on these lines would have fantastic impact. Radio Moscow after the October revolution could only say: 'We are not going to pay the Tsar's debts'. We in Britain have a powerful lever of world revolution in the vast £20 billion British capital investment abroad.

Workers in Britain can be confident that their example will be followed, or better still, surpassed, by workers in other countries. Socialists in Britain should not worry that we will be in advance of workers in other countries and isolated. On the contrary, the danger is that we will lag behind, held back by a long conservative tradition of reformism and parliamentarism.

We are entering a long period of instability. International capitalism will be rent by economic, social and political crises. Big class battles are ahead of us. Their outcome will decide the future of humanity for a long time to come.